HOW TO GET THE MOST OUT OF THIS COURSE

SUGGESTIONS FOR GROUP LEADERS

We're deliberately not prescriptive, and different leaders prefer to ⋯
are a few tried-and-trusted ideas ...

1. THE ROOM Encourage people to sit within the main circle, so that all feel equally involved.

2. HOSPITALITY Tea or coffee and biscuits on arrival and/or at the end of a meeting are always appreciated and encourage people to talk informally.

3. THE START If group members don't know one another well, some kind of 'icebreaker' might be helpful. For example, you might invite people to share something about themselves and/or their faith. Be careful to place a time limit on this exercise!

4. PREPARING THE GROUP Explain that there are no right or wrong answers, and that among friends it is fine to say things you're not sure about – to express half-formed ideas. If individuals choose to say nothing, that's all right too.

5. THE MATERIAL It helps if each group member has their own personal copy of this course book. Encourage members to read each session *before* the meeting. There's no need to consider all the questions. A lively exchange of views is what matters, so be selective. The quotations are there to stimulate discussion and – just like the opinions expressed by the audio participants – don't necessarily represent York Courses' views or beliefs.

6. PREPARATION It's not compulsory for group members to have a Bible, but you will want one. Ask in advance if you want anyone to lead prayers or read aloud, so that they can prepare.

7. TIMING Aim to start on time and stick fairly closely to your stated finishing time.

8. USING THE AUDIO/VIDEO The track markers on the audio/video (and shown on the transcript) will help you to find your way around the recorded material very easily. For each of the sessions, we recommend reading through the session in the course book, before listening together to the corresponding session on the audio material/watching the video. Groups may like to choose a question to discuss straight after they have listened to/watched a relevant track on the audio/video – but there are no hard-and-fast rules. Do whatever works best for your group!

9. THE TRANSCRIPT, included at the end of the course book, is a written record of the audio/video material and will be invaluable as you prepare. Group members will benefit from having their own copy.

RUNNING A VIRTUAL HOUSE GROUP AND SHARING AUDIO/VIDEO

To run your virtual group, use software such as Zoom or Google Meet, and use the 'Share Screen' function to share the audio/video with your group.

HOW TO DOWNLOAD THE AUDIO AND VIDEO

To access the downloadable audio that comes with the course book, go to https://www.spckpublishing. co.uk/searching-for-home-york-courses-video and use the code SearchingForHomeMP3 to purchase it for free on the site. This site also provides access to the video. For more information on how to download your audio, go to https://www.spckpublishing.co.uk/searching-for-home-york-courses-audio.

The full list of available formats is as follows:

- Course book including transcript of video and access to video/audio downloads (paperback 978 1 73918 200 7)
- Course book including transcript of video and access to video/audio downloads (eBook 978 1 915843 27 2, both ePub and Mobi files provided)
- Participants' book including transcript of video: pack of 5 (Paperback 978 1 915843 25 8)
- Participants' book including transcript of video (eBook 978 1 915843 26 5, both ePub and Mobi files provided)
- Video of discussion to support *Searching for Home*, available via the course book with access to audio and video downloads
- Audio book of discussion to support *Searching for Home* (audio digital download 978 1 915843 29 6)
- Audio book of discussion to support *Searching for Home* (CD 978 1 915843 28 9)

SEARCHING FOR HOME

Advent reflections on the God who welcomes everyone

An ecumenical course in four sessions

Cole Moreton

CONTENTS

Sessions

Transcript

SESSION 1
LEAVING HOME

In the sixth month of Elizabeth's pregnancy, God sent the angel Gabriel to Nazareth, a town in Galilee, to a virgin pledged to be married to a man named Joseph, a descendant of David. The virgin's name was Mary. The angel went to her and said, 'Greetings, you who are highly favoured! The Lord is with you.'

Mary was greatly troubled at his words and wondered what kind of greeting this might be. But the angel said to her, 'Do not be afraid, Mary; you have found favour with God. You will conceive and give birth to a son, and you are to call him Jesus. He will be great and will be called the Son of the Most High. The Lord God will give him the throne of his father David, and he will reign over Jacob's descendants for ever; his kingdom will never end.'

LUKE 1:26–33

We wait.

That's what Advent is about.

We wait for the story to begin, for the star to rise in the night sky, for the faint sound of angels singing to grow louder and for the child to be born. We wait to dress our children in wings and halos, shepherds' clothes and the finery of kings, to put on nativity plays and exchange gifts in honour of the gift of life. We wait to celebrate the birth that changed everything and, as we do, we remember all that came before it, as recorded in the Scriptures, including the prophecies, the poetry and the voices calling in the wilderness, hungry for change.

We may recognise that hunger in ourselves. We may see parallels between that time and ours, between the world as it was then and the world as it is now, between what we and others are going through now and what Mary and Joseph went through then.

The excitement at something new happening, for example. The anticipation of a new arrival.

'If you come at four in the afternoon, I'll begin to be happy by three.'
ANTOINE DE SAINT-EXUPÉRY

There's something else in this story that may resonate too. The pain of having to leave home. Countless men, women and children are experiencing that as you read this, in these days of war, famine and natural disaster. Caught up in forces beyond their control, driven out of their place of safety, made to move on against their will.

'We leave something of ourselves behind when we leave a place, we stay there, even though we go away.'
PAUL MERCIER

The first time Mary and Joseph had to leave home it was a relatively calm, ordered affair. Yes, they lived in an occupied land. Yes, the Romans had created a hostile environment, which involved telling everyone to go back to where they came from. According to the story, citizens were ordered to return to their towns and villages of origin so that their names could be recorded there. For Mary, young and heavily pregnant, that must have been a very tough journey. Ninety miles through the heat of the day and the cold of night, at first along the plains beside the river Jordan, then up into the hills around Jerusalem and finally onward to the village of Bethlehem, where Joseph still had relatives.

But at least there had been time to prepare. Time to pack what was needed and could be carried, in Joseph's arms or on his back or on a donkey.

In those days Caesar Augustus issued a decree that a census should be taken of the entire Roman world. (This was the first census that took place while Quirinius was governor of Syria.) And everyone went to their own town to register. So Joseph also went up from the town of Nazareth in Galilee to Judea, to Bethlehem the town of David, because

he belonged to the house and line of David. He went there
to register with Mary, who was pledged to be married to
him and was expecting a child.
LUKE 2:1–5

Nobody was threatening them. Yes, they were being bullied by
the state, but so was everyone. The world was moving towards a
tipping point, but nobody knew it. The wise men, far away in all
their mystery, had yet to see a star. The shepherds watched their
flocks, oblivious to gathering choirs of angels or the idea that
generations of future children would sing about them. The people
of Bethlehem went about their lives, eating and sleeping under
the same broad sky, with no sense that they were about to be
pitched into the heart of a revolutionary story. The innkeeper was
probably fussing about how to accommodate all the extra guests
coming his way because of the census.

Nobody was preparing for the birth of the actual baby except
his earthly parents: Joseph the carpenter, still not quite sure what
to think about it all, but anxious to find a place for his young wife
to lie down and gather her strength; and Mary, hoping that the
angel had been no delusion and all was as promised. Most highly
favoured lady, the angel had called her, but we might wonder,
did she really feel like that at the time?

'Mary's life shows that God accomplishes great deeds
through those who are the most humble.'
POPE FRANCIS

Mary may have been from Nazareth, but she may have been
from Sepphora or Jerusalem, according to some stories. We don't
really know. We do know that Bethlehem was her husband's home
village. So when she got there, tired after five days of travel with a
baby inside her, anxious for rest, at least physically, Mary was a
long way from home. There is evidence to suggest that the young
family would settle there for a while though, because when King
Herod was told of the birth of a boy who might threaten his reign,
he ordered his soldiers to murder every male child in Bethlehem
aged under 2. The second time Mary and Joseph had to leave
home, then, it was in a hurry, fleeing killers. It must have been

terrifying. This is a scene that gets left out of our nativity plays, not least because it's too difficult, too disturbing for young eyes and ears. It has new resonance at the moment though, because of so much that is happening in the world. We will look at this part of the story in more detail next time.

As we prepare to do so, over the coming week I would like to invite you to spend some time thinking about the image *La sagrada familia*, available at https://kellylatimoreicons.com/en-gb/products/la-sagrada-familia. It was created by the artist Kelly Latimore following a conversation with an undocumented immigrant shortly after Donald Trump had been elected President of the United States in 2016. The news at the time was full of the new president's plans to build a wall along the southern border of the USA. As the artist has said: 'We were sitting around a bonfire one night with this young man from Guatemala who told us why he was in the USA, his struggles, his hopes and fears. He had come here as a teenager, only to be deported and then almost beaten to death in Mexico. He eventually crossed the desert again to the USA. Everything about him broke us. He has the image of God within him. As we were hearing all of the hateful rhetoric that was anti-immigrant, anti-stranger, his experience immediately came to mind while creating this modern holy family image and showing how the refugees Jesus, Mary and Joseph must have felt fleeing from Herod two thousand years ago.'

'Home isn't where you're from, it's where you find light when all grows dark.'
PIERCE BROWN

What does the painting say to you? How does it make you feel? The artist has chosen to portray Mary, Joseph and Jesus in a modern situation. In which other situations might we paint them? If you had to leave home in a hurry right now, what would you take with you and where would you go? That will come up next time. These are questions you might like to consider during the week, or privately for a moment before we get to the group discussion. There's no obligation to share the answers with anyone, unless you want to.

Was there ever a moment when you had to leave home, like Mary on her donkey? How did you feel? Where did you go? Who supported you? Who was there for you? Who kept in touch with you? And when you were lonely in the new place, if you thought longingly of home as Mary must have done, who or what did you long for?

'It is an absolute human certainty that no one can know his own beauty or perceive a sense of his own worth until it has been reflected back to him in the mirror of another loving, caring human being.'
JOHN JOSEPH POWELL

Perhaps you were glad to have left. We don't all come from homes that are happy. Some of our homes are full of pain, full of challenge. Some contain harm, some are charged with sadness, some are worth leaving. Was it a relief to leave home then? Was it a liberation? Was it the start of a journey into freedom? Were you looking for a way to heal?

'It's amazing how a little tomorrow can make up for a whole lot of yesterday.'
JOHN GUARE

If that was how you felt when you were leaving, where did you find comfort? Did you ever find a different kind of home?

FOR DISCUSSION

1. What is home? What does it mean to you? Is it the place you live now or the place you were born or somewhere else entirely? Is it bricks and mortar or the memories they hold? Is it the familiar streets, shops, pubs and landscape of the place you are from? Is it the culture of the people who live there, the way they speak, the little habits they have, the food they eat? Is it the things they laugh at, the stories they tell, the music they listen to? Is it the people who are close to you? Do they constitute home? Is it your family? Is it your friends? Is it your lover or your partner?

2. What does home mean to you emotionally? Does it mean safety? Does it mean security? Does it mean comfort? Does it mean shelter? What does it mean?

3. Whatever home means to you, it is also a word that can be used to describe a kind of longing that seems part of the human condition. As Christians we might think of this as a longing for God, for the beauty of creation as it was in the beginning and the world as it should be, for our lost Eden, for the coming of God's reign and our closeness to the Creator – a kind of homesickness, without quite knowing where that home is. How do you think that longing can be satisfied in us? Where do you find rest and belonging? What are the ways in which God reaches out to give us a sense of home?

SESSION 2
FLEEING HOME

After Jesus was born in Bethlehem in Judea, during the time of King Herod, Magi from the east came to Jerusalem and asked, 'Where is the one who has been born king of the Jews? We saw his star when it rose and have come to worship him.'

When King Herod heard this he was disturbed, and all Jerusalem with him. When he had called together all the people's chief priests and teachers of the law, he asked them where the Messiah was to be born. 'In Bethlehem in Judea,' they replied, 'for this is what the prophet has written:

'"But you, Bethlehem, in the land of Judah,
    are by no means least among the rulers of Judah;
for out of you will come a ruler
    who will shepherd my people Israel."'

Then Herod called the Magi secretly and found out from them the exact time the star had appeared. He sent them to Bethlehem and said, 'Go and search carefully for the child. As soon as you find him, report to me, so that I too may go and worship him.'

After they had heard the king, they went on their way, and the star they had seen when it rose went ahead of them until it stopped over the place where the child was. When they saw the star, they were overjoyed. On coming to the house, they saw the child with his mother Mary, and they bowed down and worshipped him. Then they opened their treasures and presented him with gifts of gold, frankincense and myrrh. And having been warned in a dream not to go back to Herod, they returned to their country by another route.

When they had gone, an angel of the Lord appeared to Joseph in a dream. 'Get up,' he said, 'take the child and his mother and escape to Egypt. Stay there until I tell you, for Herod is going to search for the child to kill him.'

So he got up, took the child and his mother during the night and left for Egypt, where he stayed until the death of Herod. And so was fulfilled what the Lord had said through the prophet: 'Out of Egypt I called my son.'
MATTHEW 2:1–15

Joseph woke in the night with a burning conviction that they should leave. Now. Right now. No more waiting. Go.

He was nobody famous, nobody controversial, not a politician or a rebel leader, just a small-town carpenter with a young wife and son who had lived quietly among relatives in Bethlehem for a year or so after the birth, without much money but with a sense of purpose and care. Joseph woke with the knowledge that soldiers were coming for the child. To find and kill him. How did he know? An angel told him, the Bible says. It was in a dream. Just a dream. Ask yourself now, would you trust that if it happened to you? Would you get up and run on the basis of a vivid dream? Or would you say it was the side effect of a bad night's sleep, the worries on your mind or last night's meal? Would you laugh it off? Put it out of your mind? Forget about it, get on with your day, until it was too late?

'Dreams are divine gems.
Find and keep them safe.'
MICHAEL BASSEY JOHNSON

We know Joseph had listened to his dreams before and acted on them. When Mary had somehow got pregnant without him, Joseph had been told in a dream that it was God's will. This must have been confusing or alarming, but he trusted the words. He stood by the girl. So much that happened afterwards may have felt like confirmation that something was happening in his life that was extraordinary, beyond the edge of understanding. The bright star in the sky, the angels that seemed to fill the air, the learned men who brought gifts for the baby. Now this, though.

'Get up,' the angel said. 'Take the child and his mother and escape to Egypt.'

So Joseph did. It's easy to imagine him waking Mary, stumbling over his words, frightening her with the urgency of his voice and the wildness in his eyes, getting her to understand that, yes, it had to be now, right now. Then packing a bag, quickly. Gathering up their things and the child and slipping out of the house under cover of darkness, feeling the chill in the night air, listening for the sound of troops approaching, watching for the lights of burning torches, breathing quick and shallow; urging Mary on, holding her hand, looking into her eyes and trying to give her some sense of calm, only silently for fear of being heard.

'No one leaves home unless home is the mouth of a shark.'
WARSAN SHIRE

And Mary, what did she make of it all? A young woman of immense strength and purpose, strong enough to give birth to a child who carried the hopes of the world, she was also still a teenager, still growing, being rushed from sleep to flee in fear. There must have been tears, surely, for both Mary and Joseph, and for the baby, disturbed and feeling the rush of cold. They took what they could carry and they ran, then walked, for more days and nights and days. They must have been scared, shaken, full of worry, exhausted, as they worked their way beyond the reach of Herod, down along the Way of the Sea into Egypt, where their ancestors had lived in exile and where there was still a Jewish community, people among whom they might find shelter and kindness. Perhaps. They were moving towards a future they could not yet see, because Joseph was convinced the boy would be murdered otherwise. And he was right.

When Herod realised that he had been outwitted by the Magi, he was furious, and he gave orders to kill all the boys in Bethlehem and its vicinity who were two years old and under, in accordance with the time he had learned from the Magi. Then what was said through the prophet Jeremiah was fulfilled:

'A voice is heard in Ramah,
weeping and great mourning,
Rachel weeping for her children
and refusing to be comforted,
because they are no more.'
MATTHEW 2:16–18

In this moment, were the holy family refugees?

The question has become controversial in recent times, because of the hostile attitudes taken up by governments in the UK and the USA. If you're a person of faith whose leaders are inclined to show no mercy to those seeking refuge, it is challenging to realise that Jesus himself was once in that position. However, when we look at the reasons why Mary and Joseph fled to Egypt with the boy, the answer has to be yes. They were refugees, by the modern definition.

'Home is a notion that only nations of the homeless fully appreciate and only the uprooted comprehend.'
WALLACE STEGNER

Herod was a ruthless ruler with a secret police and a huge bodyguard, but he was also very much afraid of insurrection. It was the Romans who had named him King of the Jews, not the people of Judea. He had built fortresses and restored the temple, but he still feared rebellion. That's why he asked the wise men to tell him where he could find this young boy they were talking about, the one who would apparently one day be king.

When the wise men scarpered instead, he was furious.

Mary, Joseph and Jesus fled their home to avoid being caught up in a massacre, the motive for which was politics, or rather Herod's burning desire to keep power. They left Judea and went to Egypt, where the king had no jurisdiction.

'The good man is free, even if he is a slave. The evil man is a slave, even if he is a king.'
ST AUGUSTINE

'Isn't it kind of silly to think that tearing someone else down builds you up?'
SEAN COVEY

True, it was all part of the Roman Empire and it's hard to make direct comparisons between the situation then and the nation states we have now, but listen to what the United Nations High Commission for Refugees (UNHCR) says and consider whether some or all of this applied to that little family striking out in the dark. 'Refugees are people who have fled war, violence, conflict or persecution and have crossed an international border to find safety in another country. They often have had to flee with little more than the clothes on their back, leaving behind homes, possessions, jobs and loved ones. Refugees are defined and protected in international law. The 1951 Refugee Convention is a key legal document and defines a refugee as: "someone who is unable or unwilling to return to their country of origin owing to a well-founded fear of being persecuted for reasons of race, religion, nationality, membership of a particular social group, or political opinion".'

That definition currently applies to 27.1 million people around the world.

'Give me your tired, your poor, your huddled masses yearning to breathe free.'
EMMA LAZARUS

The Russian invasion of Ukraine has caused more than 7.8 million people to flee within Europe since February 2022, according to the UNHCR. More than 6.5 million are believed to have been displaced inside Ukraine.

Millions of Syrians have been forced to flee their homes since 2011, seeking safety as refugees in Lebanon, Turkey, Jordan and beyond, or displaced inside Syria. There are more than 943,000 Rohinga refugees in Bangladesh.

A full-scale humanitarian crisis is unfolding because of fighting in northern Ethiopia's Tigray region, says the UNHCR as another example. 'Since the violence began in early November 2020, refugees have been arriving at remote border points that take hours to reach from the nearest towns in Sudan. Many are women and children. Most left with barely any belongings and arrived exhausted from walking long distances over harsh terrain. With no end in sight to the conflict, the steady stream of daily arrivals is overwhelming the current capacity to provide aid. More support is urgently needed.'

They move like Mary, Joseph and Jesus. There are currently nearly 60,000 refugees from Ethiopia in Sudan.

In a sense, though, the numbers do not matter. The individuals count. If every man, every woman and every child is loved by God, should those of us who are able to do so not therefore love and care for them too?

'Let's think of the many people who are victims of wars, who want to flee from their homeland but cannot; let's think of the migrants who set out on the road to freedom but end up on the street or in the sea; let's think of Jesus in the arms of Joseph and Mary, fleeing, and let us see in him each one of the migrants of today.'
POPE FRANCIS, December 2021

'Christ asks for a home in your soul, where he can be at rest with you, where he can talk easily to you, where you and he, alone together, can laugh and be silent and be delighted with one another.'
CARYLL HOUSELANDER

FOR DISCUSSION

1. How would you handle a situation like this? Would you trust your own instincts? What if the voice of the angel was carried by the news, coming over on the radio or the television, rising up in the murmurs of neighbours or flashing up on your phone? Would you go then, or would you wait to see what happened? Would you be pleased to have a warning or dismiss the talk of trouble as

fear-mongering? Would you take a chance on it all blowing over? Would you wait until you could hear the explosions, see the rocket vapour trails, feel the approach of tanks?

2. If everything you consider safe was no longer safe and you had to run, where would you run to? Who would you call? What if you had no way to call anyone, no way to make plans, you just had to leave?

3. Think about this as a real, present emergency, happening in this moment. What do you take? Come on, you need to leave. What's in your bag? Who's coming with you? Where are you going? How are you getting there? Where might there be shelter? Somewhere they speak your language? Somewhere you might have relatives, if you can find them? There's no time to think. You've got to go. Now. What's the first thing you do?

SESSION 3
CARRYING HOME

He told them: 'Take nothing for the journey – no staff, no bag, no bread, no money, no extra shirt. Whatever house you enter, stay there until you leave that town. If people do not welcome you, leave their town and shake the dust off your feet as a testimony against them.'
LUKE 9:3–5

So you've got to go. What will you take?

Your passport yes, you'll need that. Life is very difficult for a refugee, but even more so for a refugee without papers. You are going to need to prove who you are. Come on, let's get going. Medicines – you need to stay alive. Money, maybe, if you have any. Your phone, yes, while it's still got charge. Everything is on there, right? The numbers of the people you love and the people who will help you. Information. Music that reminds you of this home you're leaving in a hurry.

Photographs, of course. The faces, the smiles, the happy times. The memories. They're all on there. Hold tight to that phone, your world is shrinking to the size of a handset. What else is in your rucksack? Food for the journey, more clothes to keep warm, a hat, scarves, gloves, who knows? Grab whatever you can.

Time is up.

Let's go.

'My cell phone is my best friend. It's my lifeline to the outside world.'
CARRIE UNDERWOOD

Jesus told his friends to take nothing with them when they went out into the world, and they may well have been shocked by that, but he must have grown up knowing the story of the night his parents fled. The night they were, in our modern language, refugees.

The photographer Kiki Streitberger was so touched by the migration of hundreds of thousands of displaced men, women and children across the Mediterranean to Europe that she sought out those refugees and their stories and began to ask about the possessions they were carrying with them as reminders of home. The result was a deeply moving exhibition called Travelling Light, for which she photographed the contents of their bags and recorded their words. It can be seen at https://kikistreitberger. com/portfolio/travelling-light/.

Ahmad, a 40-year-old printer who had owned his own supermarket in Syria, brought creams to help with chafing on the journey and sea sickness pills that didn't work. He brought a few notes of old Syrian currency, worthless now except to him. 'I brought it because it reminds me of home and my shop and my friends who came to visit me.' His bag also contained an old, empty lighter from his supermarket. 'It's now broken, but I still want to keep it as a memory.'

'Sometimes memory is the only gift we give ourselves and the only hope we have of finding our way home.'
HARLEY KING

Shahed, a 5-year-old from Syria, brought a doll with bright pink clothes and straw-blonde hair. 'She is called Aia. She is my friend. My dad gave her to me. I've had her since I was one year old. She sleeps in my bed with me every night. She is so cute.' Shahed and Aia had travelled from Damascus to Egypt, to Libya, across the sea to Italy and on to Germany.

Hecmet, a 49-year-old housewife, brought a small metal falafel-maker from home. 'I didn't expect to find one abroad.'

Mohammed, a 32-year-old computer programmer, brought prayer beads that had belonged to his mother. 'I miss my mum and I think of her when I hold the beads.'

'Home is where somebody notices when you are no longer there.'
ALEKSANDAR HEMON

Aloa, a student aged 14, brought an asthma inhaler, a notebook, a book on Arabic history, a pair of glasses and his last school report. 'I brought it with me because I want to show people that I'm not stupid. When I come and ask for asylum this doesn't mean I am an idiot and I want people to know that.'

Not all the baggage that refugees carry is visible. There are also emotions, memories, mental burdens. Wais, who was only 6, said: 'I can remember the ships very well. I was feeling so sick and was throwing up all the time. They threw us from one ship to another in the middle of the sea. One ship was made of wood and the other one was made of metal and they kept crashing together. I still have nightmares about it.'

'The most valuable possession you can own is an open heart. The most powerful weapon you can be is an instrument of peace.'
CARLOS SANTANA

Kiki Streitberger spoke to those who had arrived in Germany. I have had the privilege of meeting young men and women who came across the Channel on small boats during the early days of the current situation, before the numbers crossing rose to thousands. They were teenagers being helped by a charity in Folkestone, Kent. One of them was a bright, clever and determined Kurd called Akoy. He was from Sardasht, the town at the foot of the Zagros mountains where Saddam Hussein once dropped chemical weapons on innocent civilians and where Iranian and Kurdish forces have fought in more recent times.

'I can't go back there, it is too dangerous,' he told me. 'I am glad to talk about this because I want to get these bad memories out of my head.'

We all carry mental baggage. The things we have seen and heard and felt. The abuse done to us. The suffering we have witnessed. The loss of loved ones. The hug of a parent. The scent of a lover. The pain of separation. The tastes of home. The food we used to love, which reminds us of then and there. Akoy wants to be a cook, he wants to share those tastes with others. He hopes that will help him make new friends, find a community, make a life.

What if this was you?

'There is no pain so great as the memory of joy in present grief.'
AESCHYLUS

Akoy was 15 years old when a people-smuggler deceived him. 'The man told me lots of lies. He said: "I will send you by big boat, like the ferries they have in Dover. You will have everything you need on the boat: food, drink, everything."'

The group were driven to a remote beach. The rain was lashing down in the darkness and the wind was high. 'We were scared when we saw this three-metre rubber boat. There were twenty-two of us. We had to unpack it from a box and pump the boat up by hand. It took three hours. I said: "Why did you lie to me? I'm not going." He said: "You must go. I won't give your money back." I thought: if I don't go, what will I do? This is all the money we have.'

Through waves and clouds and storms,
He gently clears the way;
wait thou His time; so shall this night
soon end in joyous day.
PAUL GERHARDT, tr. JOHN WESLEY

So Akoy got on, but the boat turned over in the surf and threw them out, once, then twice and a third time. They were soaked. It was two in the morning. 'We could see one red light on the other side. The smuggler told the one they made the driver: "Don't worry. Just aim for that."' They set off, but the boat filled up quickly. They were scooping out the water with a bucket, for hours. 'I was very scared.' He makes a hand motion to show the boat rising and falling on the waves. 'I think I am dead. Everybody thought they were dead. We said a prayer, the one that Muslims say when we are dying. The Afghan people texted their families to say goodbye. I would have texted my brother but I didn't have my phone.'

As the boat began to sink, the one in charge had thrown some of the bags overboard, to try to keep them all afloat.

Akoy's phone was gone. Think about that.

If nothing else, we have our phones. The numbers that matter to us. The apps we need to gain access to money or health information. The photographs of our friends and family and loved ones, the old life, the dog, the mountains.

And then it's gone. Lost in the waves.

Nothing to hold. Nobody to contact. Nothing to see.

What then? What have you got then?

Your faith? Really?

What would that mean to you in that moment, if you thought you were about to die? What would you pray?

'When the time comes that some of us will have to die, you will look into your heart and find the strength you need – just in time.'
CORRIE TEN BOOM

'The safest place in all the world is to be sheltered in the love of God.'
CHARLES RINGMA

And what does it do to you, thinking about these questions?

How does it make you feel about Akoy, Wais, Aloa, Shahed and the others?

Aren't they just like you? Just like the people you love?

Aren't they loved too?

'"For I was hungry and you gave me something to eat, I was thirsty and you gave me something to drink, I was a stranger and you invited me in, I needed clothes and you clothed me, I was sick and you looked after me, I was in prison and you came to visit me."

'Then the righteous will answer him, "Lord, when did we see you hungry and feed you, or thirsty and give you something to drink? When did we see you a stranger and invite you in, or needing clothes and clothe you? When did we see you sick or in prison and go to visit you?"

'The King will reply, "Truly I tell you, whatever you did for one of the least of these brothers and sisters of mine, you did for me."'
MATTHEW 25:35–40

Who was Jesus talking to here? What was the story he was telling?

Who did he mean by 'the least of these'? Who would we describe in that way now?

This country is not welcoming to refugees, officially. There is one big exception that we will come to in a moment, but for the most part the government's approach to those seeking asylum has been set for more than a decade by what Theresa May said when she was Prime Minister in May 2012: 'The aim is to create here in Britain a really hostile environment for illegal migration.' Landlords, employers, work colleagues and NHS staff were encouraged to report anybody they did not think had a right to be here and vans were driven around London with posters saying: 'Go home or face arrest.' This may seem reasonable, if laws are being broken. The trouble is the huge number of people who are being left in limbo by the system, waiting to see if their applications for asylum will be approved or not. At the time of writing, the Home Office has a crisis on its hands with a backlog of more than 166,000 cases. Some of those have been waiting for years.

While they are waiting, they are given a place to stay and an allowance of £45 a week for food, clothing and toiletries, which drops down to £9.10 a week if their accommodation provides breakfast and dinner. Some will say this is generous. It is more than some countries provide and less than others. The trouble is that the usual British assumption that you are innocent until proven guilty seems to be overturned in the case of asylum seekers. Anwar said: 'When I was in Afghanistan, I was always called by my name, but in Europe suddenly they changed my name to refugee. I am a human before a refugee.'

Even as I write this, there is someone on the radio saying that they're all economic migrants, not fleeing war or persecution at all. However, Home Office figures suggest otherwise. According to the most recent release, only 23 per cent of applicants are rejected. Of those, a third win their case on appeal. That means the vast majority of people who apply for asylum are eventually accepted as legitimate refugees. Nevertheless, the government continues to act as if the opposite is true. It is persisting with the plan to fly asylum seekers to Rwanda even before their claims have been looked at, despite opposition in the European Court of Human Rights.

The Home Secretary, Suella Braverman, has called the increasing numbers of people coming across the Channel on small boats an invasion. That is a powerful word with strong echoes in history. She used it just a few days after firebombs were thrown at a migrant processing centre in Dover. The charity Care4Calais called her language 'highly offensive' while Refugee Action said it would put lives at risk. Other politicians also continue to talk about asylum seekers as if they are aliens, a menace and the enemy, which inflames opinion, sometimes literally.

'The need to belong to yourself, the deepest need of all, can only be fulfilled through the beautiful force-field of friendship.'
JOHN O'DONOHUE

A crowd of protesters gathered outside a hotel on Merseyside where asylum seekers were staying in early 2023, set fire to a police van and chanted: 'Get them out!' The crowd had taken exception to the alleged actions of one of the residents, although a charity worker on the scene said: 'There are people who have committed crimes in nearby Walton prison but nobody says the whole population of Liverpool are criminals.' An asylum seeker who had been a teacher in his war-torn home country and was now staying in the hotel while he waited for his claim to be processed told a reporter: 'We haven't done anything wrong; we just came here to try to be safe and it is not safe.'

Anyone who does get refugee status may feel like celebrating, but they will also have their accommodation and payments taken away with immediate effect, which can leave them homeless and desperate. Charities, councils and church groups across the country have set up schemes to help people to get through this difficult time and make the applications that will enable them to work and find somewhere to live.

'Do all the good you can,
by all the means you can,
in all the ways you can,
in all the places you can,
at all the times you can,
to all the people you can,
as long as ever you can.'
JOHN WESLEY

People are much more generous than the system – that's the obvious truth. When the small boats first began to come, it was fishermen who often found them. I went out into the open sea on one trawler to see what it was like for a Radio 4 documentary, and the skipper told me with tears in his eyes about the time he came across an overladen boat whose occupants included a very small child. They were soaked through, chilled to the bone, shaking and fearful for their lives, as the water was coming in and the vessel was sinking. At the time, there were politicians calling for the navy to shoot at the boats and sink them, to deter any more from coming, but he thought this was inhuman. He said: 'Won't they all drown? And how could anyone with a heart see a woman with her baby out here in these conditions and not immediately want to help?'

'To save a life is a real and beautiful thing. To make a home for the homeless, yes, it is a thing that must be good; whatever the world may say, it cannot be wrong.'
VINCENT VAN GOGH

I've also spoken to teenagers who were children when they made the crossing, and it is striking how some of them talk about the gentleness with which the Border Force and police officers treated them in contrast to the way they had been beaten or verbally abused by authorities in other countries. Those teenagers are often placed with foster parents, who offer care. There is also, as I said, one obvious exception to all the official hostility. Thousands of men, women and children from Ukraine have been welcomed into homes since Russia invaded in February 2022, treated as guests and become friends. This wonderful expression of compassion and solidarity on the part of the British people has been matched by the attitude of the government, which has made life much easier for them than for others who come here. For example Anastasia Shlyakhtyna, a lawyer and aid worker, was given an emergency three-year visa along with 100,000 others from Ukraine and was able to find work and earn money to support herself and her 10-year-old son: 'We are so grateful to the people of London for the generous hospitality they have shown us. We have lost so much in this war but to have the city welcome us with open arms and offer my children a place in school gives me so much hope for the future. I'm from Mariupol and my city is destroyed. I lost everything. But I am so in love with London and the UK.'

This is truly heart-warming, but it also raises questions. Let's talk about those and others now.

FOR DISCUSSION

1. Why has there been such an outpouring of love for Ukrainian refugees when others – such as the victims of war in Syria – have not been treated in the same way? What is it that makes one

group of people in need apparently acceptable and another not so much?

2. There have been so many great examples of generosity and welcome on the part of individuals, groups and churches. Which ones can you think of in your area? Which have touched you personally? The idea of refugees and asylum seekers being housed in hotels attracts a lot of opposition, but where should they go, if not there? As for the boats, there is a very real and pressing problem with the people-smugglers who are exploiting desperate people and putting lives in danger, but what would you do if you were in charge? Would you try to close the borders? Would you throw them open instead?

3. As we think about the holy family in exile in Egypt and the transforming life of Christ – who defied the conventions of his day, sat with the unloved, kneeled down to children and spoke up for those in trouble – we may ask ourselves: what would Jesus do, here and now? Where would he be? Who would he be with? What would Jesus have us do for that person?

SESSION 4
FINDING HOME

When Joseph and Mary had done everything required by the Law of the Lord, they returned to Galilee to their own town of Nazareth. And the child grew and became strong; he was filled with wisdom, and the grace of God was on him.

Every year Jesus' parents went to Jerusalem for the Festival of the Passover. When he was twelve years old, they went up to the festival, according to the custom. After the festival was over, while his parents were returning home, the boy Jesus stayed behind in Jerusalem, but they were unaware of it. Thinking he was in their company, they travelled on for a day. Then they began looking for him among their relatives and friends. When they did not find him, they went back to Jerusalem to look for him. After three days they found him in the temple courts, sitting among the teachers, listening to them and asking them questions. Everyone who heard him was amazed at his understanding and his answers. When his parents saw him, they were astonished. His mother said to him, 'Son, why have you treated us like this? Your father and I have been anxiously searching for you.'

'Why were you searching for me?' he asked. 'Didn't you know I had to be in my Father's house?' But they did not understand what he was saying to them.

Then he went down to Nazareth with them and was obedient to them. But his mother treasured all these things in her heart.
LUKE 2:39–51

The nativity is one of those stories in which the future looms large, as the shadow of the cross falls on the manger. We have been looking ahead all through this course and we will do so again today. As the Christmas lights shine in the fourth week of Advent and we prepare to gather to celebrate the birth of this boy who changed the world – who changes our world every day – we also think of the life he was to lead. What can we learn from him about the search for home?

'The child is the beauty of God present in the world, that greatest gift to a family.'
MOTHER TERESA

The Gospels don't actually say much about the holy family's home life. We think that Mary, Jesus and Joseph returned to Nazareth when Jesus was about 4, but there is very little known about his childhood. We know he went missing when he was 12, as Luke describes in this passage. Some scholars also think that Jesus would have been initiated into the life of a carpenter like Joseph at the age of 12 and as a result may have left home, possibly to live in Capernaum.

'And suddenly you know: it's time to start something new and trust the magic of beginnings.'
MEISTER ECKHART

In later life, when he does come back into view through the Gospel accounts, Jesus doesn't talk much about home, on the face of it. He says that those who want to follow him need to leave their home and family to do so. He says in Matthew 8:20 that he himself does not have a home: 'Foxes have dens and birds have nests, but the Son of Man has nowhere to lay his head.' This is an accurate description of his travels from town to town, but it also feels like a reference back to the earliest memories of his life, when he was effectively on the run with his parents.

'Sometimes the strength within you is not a big fiery flame for all to see. It can be a tiny spark that whispers ever so softly, "You got this. Keep going."'
UNKNOWN

On the other hand, Jesus tells a beautiful story about a rebel son who sets off for a distant country, squanders his wealth on all sorts of shenanigans and ends up living in the muck among pigs, before coming to his senses and deciding to swallow his pride and return home. The story of the prodigal son contains a homecoming scene worthy of the end of a Hollywood film, when the father who has missed him so much sees him coming from far away, runs to him, throws his arms around the boy become man and kisses him. All is forgiven and the father brings him home. The son is welcomed unconditionally, as someone who belongs there and not as a guest. The best clothes are brought out for him, the best food is cooked. The other son, the elder of the two, is angry at this treatment, having stayed to work hard while his brother was away living the high life. He doesn't think it's fair. But maybe he's missed what home is and has to be persuaded to come and join in the celebration. The family is complete again, as far as the father is concerned. The son who was lost has been found. He's back. He's home. There's such a strong sense in this story of what home can be.

What would you say it tells us? Who do you identify with in the story? Are there broken relationships that have affected your sense of home? Is there anything we can learn from the way the father opens his arms, practises generosity and offers hospitality, along with forgiveness and healing?

'As a self-rejecting person always in search of affirmation and affection, I find it impossible to love consistently without asking for something in return.'
HENRI J. M. NOUWEN

I have learned much, personally, from meeting a teenager called Zahra and hearing her story, which is extraordinary. It reminds me of ancient folk tales in which the hero or heroine has to travel miles in search of a goal, overcoming obstacles, evading giants, facing challenges and finally making it through. Zahra was born in exile; she grew up among a million other people from Afghanistan who had been forced by war to live in Iran. 'We were not allowed to go to school, we were not allowed to go to work, you just had to live as an illegal person,' she tells me. Zahra watched planes make trails across the sky and wondered what it would be like to fly.

'If birds can glide for long periods of time, then ... why can't
I?'
WRIGHT BROTHERS

Life became dangerous in Iran, so Zahra and her mother set off
to try to make it to somewhere else. A place of promise, where
they could belong at last. A place of safety. They walked over
the mountains to Turkey and paid agents to help them cross the
Aegean, although the safe passage they paid for was not what
they were given. An eyewitness in the camps along the coast said
at the time: 'You can hear the screams of people being forced on
to these boats, often using tremendous violence. The smugglers are
armed, they have cattle prods, they put the people on the boat and
then they tell one of the refugees to steer the boat, often in complete
darkness. Many boats end up in trouble, all the time.' Zahra and
her mother made it to the other side and found themselves in a
camp in Lesbos among many displaced people. It was dangerous.
Zahra was 15. Men circled her. Zahra's mother was terrified of
them. She contacted her family, now scattered across continents,
and money was found to give Zahra a chance of going on. Zahra
crossed Europe to Paris, then travelled on to Dunkirk, then finally to
the shores of the Channel, the last great obstacle on her 7,000-mile
journey. She arrived quietly with others on the shores of Kent as the
dawn broke one Christmas morning. I met Zahra at a drop-in centre
in Folkestone, where young people like her are given friendship
and support, language lessons and help in negotiating the new
culture they now live in. Zahra has been given refugee status, which
means that for the first time in her entire life she has a right to be
somewhere. A place to live, legitimately. She has friends, a place to
live, a college to go to and the right to work and earn money. She's
studying hard and has a dream. To fly. Not just metaphorically or in
story terms: she wants to be a pilot.

'The most luxurious possession, the richest treasure anybody
has, is his personal dignity.'
JACKIE ROBINSON

And there's a twist to this tale, because one of the workers at the
project happened to run into someone who heard about Zahra's

desire to fly and took it seriously. They paid for a flying lesson and persuaded others to do the same. It will take a long time and there are difficulties still ahead but the hope is that one day she will take an apprentice degree in the aviation industry and maybe get her wings. One clear summer's morning not long ago, a Piper Archer plane took off from Lydd airfield in Kent with a flying instructor at the helm and Zahra by her side. They flew along the coast to Folkestone, until the moment when the aircraft was directly above the beach where the young girl had scrambled ashore that Christmas morning, confused about where she was and what would happen next. She had returned but with a completely different perspective, looking down from out of the blue sky as she had always dreamed. And the instructor checked her hands were on the joystick and said, calmly: 'You have control.'

We will come to our last set of discussion questions in a moment, but before we do, here are some things to ponder on your own for a moment, privately. Who do you have who believes in you like the people around Zahra believe in her? Could you offer the same love and support to someone? Are you struggling for a sense of home yourself? What would you need to feel a sense of home again?

'When you learn to love and let yourself be loved, you come home to the hearth of your own spirit. You are warm and sheltered. You are completely at one in the house of your own longing and belonging.'
JOHN O'DONOHUE

Like a refugee standing scared at the water's edge, like Zahra in the camp and like Mary at the foot of the cross, we know we will go through difficult, even devastating, times. The Bible tells us that God never stops believing in us. Deuteronomy 31:8 says: 'The LORD himself goes before you and will be with you; he will never leave you nor forsake you.' John 14:18 says that Jesus told his friends: 'I will not leave you as orphans; I will come to you.' And 1 John 4:16 says: 'And so we know and rely on the love God has for us. God is love. Whoever lives in love lives in God, and God in them.'

If we trust these words, can we begin to feel a sense of belonging, community and support that is something like being at home, wherever we are? Can we give the same to others? Can we help them find a purpose, a place to belong and a way to feel at home?

O God, you bring
hope out of emptiness
energy out of fear
new life out of grief and loss;

comfort all who have lost their homes
through persecution, war, exile,
or deliberate destruction.

Give them security,
a place to live,
and neighbours they trust
to be, with them,
a new sign of peace to the world.
JANET MORLEY (used with permission)

FOR DISCUSSION

1. Since the first week when we looked at what home meant to us, are there any ways in which your perception of this has changed? What does Jesus say to us when he tells his followers to leave their home and go with him? Is there a possibility that home makes us too comfortable, creates assumptions that close us off from the world and excludes other people from our lives? It also makes us feel safe, warm, secure and can allow us to build community and offer hospitality. Is there a balance to be struck between exile and home? Where are we on that spectrum? Where are you?

2. Are there things that those who have a sense of home can learn from those who do not? How can you embrace the life stories of those whose patterns of home and exile are very different from yours?

3. Thinking of the things we have discussed in previous weeks, what do you carry with you that reminds you of who you are, where you've come from and what you might be? Are they mementos of the past such as the precious keepsakes in a refugee's rucksack? Are they memories and promises such as the things the Bible says Mary kept close to her heart and remembered always, which would comfort and protect her in the difficult years to come?

4. As we come to the end of our time together, let's think about how all these things we have considered and felt can be turned into practical action. How can you as a group or church open your doors more widely to those who may not feel they belong among you? And what can you do personally to help someone who longs for a sense of home?

TRANSCRIPT
TRACK NUMBERS

Audio		**Video**
00	Opening credits	
01	Introduction	Introduction no subs; Introduction with subs
02	Session 1	Session 1 Leaving home no subs; Session 1 Leaving home with subs
03	Session 2	Session 2 Fleeing home no subs; Session 2 Fleeing home with subs
04	Session 3	Session 3 Carrying home no subs; Session 3 Carrying home with subs
05	Session 4	Session 4 Finding home no subs; Session 4 Finding home with subs
06	Closing credits	

TRANSCRIPT
INTRODUCTION

COLE   Hello, I'm Cole Moreton. I'm a writer and broadcaster, interested in the way we live and the things we believe. I live on the south coast of England, and I've been very aware over the last few years of the growing number of men, women and children, coming across the Channel in small boats to seek refuge here.

I'm delighted to have been asked to explore the story of the struggles faced by Mary, Joseph and the baby Jesus for this Advent course, with an eye on the situations we see all around us today. Thank you for joining us. Over the next four sessions, I'll be putting questions to Rose Hudson-Wilkin, the Bishop of Dover, Bridget Chapman, an activist who's worked with refugees here in Kent, where we're recording, and is now with the national charity Reset, and Grmalem Gonetse Kasa, who came to this country from Eritrea a number of years ago and is currently studying Fine Art at university in Canterbury. We're all meeting here for the first time. Could you introduce yourself and tell us a little bit about who you are, what you do, and also what you think of when you think of home?

Bishop Rose, shall we start with you?

ROSE   When I think of home, I think of love. I can see the faces of the people who I know love me and care about me and are wishing the best for me and, and food! Oh, food, yes, food that is highly seasoned and it's tasty. And just the gathering, the gathering of people, the, the joy, the ... you know, not having to explain yourself, but just being.

COLE   I want to come to dinner at your house! And you're currently Bishop of Dover?

ROSE   I am, indeed.

COLE   How is that, and what does that entail for you?

ROSE   The Bishop of Dover is not just a bishop *in* Dover, but actually takes on the responsibility of all of Canterbury diocese on behalf of the Archbishop of Canterbury, who, of course, *is* the diocesan bishop for the Canterbury diocese. So, I cover the diocese in my role, doing all the things that bishops do – leading, preaching, being, walking alongside, prophetically speaking.

COLE   Wonderful. Thank you.

Grmalem, how about you?

GRMALEM   Thinking home, it's a mother? Like as the Rose Bishop said, where everyone gather and have just love or life that you never think for the next minute it comes? You just thinking of the moment you are in. As like God said, you do not worry about tomorrow. You do not worry in, technically, in your brain, because you are at home, for the next comes. Because home is love of like a mother. If I have to explain of like home or mother, it won't have a word to explain of. It is a huge. And it's not been written ...

COLE   Wonderful.

GRMALEM   ... to be excellent.

COLE   Wonderful answer. I said that you were studying at university. What else are you up to?

GRMALEM   I'm Youth Ambassador at KRAN to help the young people with their basic English or basic lives in this new country, in new home that arrive, which I really great with KRAN and appreciate how they welcome. And that's our next home – that's our second home. We felt like our right. We found this, and I am there to help the young people as well.

COLE   And KRAN is Kent Refugee Action Network, which is where I met Bridget. Bridget Chapman, tell me who you are and what you're doing and what you think of home.

BRIDGET   So, I'm Bridget, and when I think of home, I think of being by the sea. I'm a Londoner by birth, but I grew up abroad in lots of different places. But usually by the sea. And now, for me, home is anywhere if I'm by the sea with a big sky. I've been here in Kent for nine years now and I feel very at home here on the Kent coast. And when I first got here, I got a job working for Kent Refugee Action Network, which works with people who've arrived as unaccompanied asylum-seeking children, which is where I was lucky enough to meet Grmalem and many other young people.
And obviously, Kent has been very much in the foreground of the arrival of small boats. And in amongst all of that, I've tried to help people who've made that journey. I've tried to be an advocate for them and to give them some kind of a voice because I think that we don't always hear their voices, and their voices are the most important in this debate.

COLE   And you currently work with another charity?

BRIDGET   I work with a charity called Reset, which is the national refugee charity that nobody has ever heard of, but I work in communications, so it's my job to make sure that people have heard of them. And what they do is they work with people that arrive through official resettlement routes. So, it's much less controversial than the work that I was doing with KRAN. But I think everybody around this table, and I think almost everybody I've ever met, would agree that everybody's entitled to a *safe* journey from one place to another. And what we aim to do is to give the option to more and more people.

COLE   Thank you. And we'll be picking up on themes that you've all brought up in your description as we go on with this chat.

SESSION 1
LEAVING HOME

COLE   Our experiences of leaving home, and indeed what constitutes home for us, will vary greatly. Bishop Rose, when you were young, you had a clear call to leave Jamaica and come to the UK to train as an evangelist. Maybe you could share some of your thoughts or feelings on Mary's encounter with the angel Gabriel and the tough journey to Bethlehem that followed?

How have you seen their experiences echoed in the lives of the people you care for as Bishop of Dover?

ROSE   For me, it was a surprise, in as much as Mary's call was also a surprise. It comes out of the blue, as it were, this deep inner thing that tells you that this is real. And so, with faith and hope, you trust that voice, that calling, and you say yes, as Mary did, and we're going to follow through on that.

And I think for many, whether they're younger in terms of being children, or the adults, they're at a point where something tells them deep inside that where they are is no longer safe. And so, there is almost this inner compulsion that we have to do something different; we have to make the change for the sake of our offsprings, our family, or even one's own life.

And that's not an easy decision to arrive at, because there is all that is being left behind. You are leaving behind family and friends, so there's a deep sense of loss. You're travelling forward, but you are feeling that sense of loss, whether it be family, whether it be friends, and there is also the fact that it is unknown.

You don't know how you're going to be received, where you're going to live, whether the path is going to be clear for you. So, you are leaving with a sense of hope, yes, but there is some trauma in that. You know, I can recall when I was taken to the airport, my first time leaving Jamaica, you know, I went through immigration, and I was just overwhelmed. I was crying my eyes out. And then I said, 'Can I go back out? I just need to go back out!' And I gave my dad, my adopted dad, this great big hug, and he said, 'You'd better get back in there, Rose!' So, there is this sense of mental and emotional scarring from this journey that you believe that you are being called to go on, and you do it because something inside you says, yes, this is the right thing to do. But it is not an easy journey. There is a lot of trauma, there is a lot of pain, there is a lot of uncertainty. There's nothing certain and sure about the path that you're about to step off on to.

COLE Bridget and Grmalem, some of what Rose has just said must really echo with you.

GRMALEM It does! It just like, I shouldn't be here! [*Laughs*] Obviously, the way you have understand of that and you haven't seen war ... I couldn't say it in English, but I have to say it in my language, which said [*Speaks phrase*] which someone hasn't been in the war. But when people came from the war and he's been bright, say like, 'Oh, you should do this, you should do this, you should do this.' And because he hasn't been there, he's just trying to tell them what they should do, you know? Which they ...

COLE Yeah.

GRMALEM He's trying to be bright, you know?

COLE Right, right.

GRMALEM But because he wasn't in that war. But you know that, you know, you just like, even though you haven't been crossed that, and you flew there from Jamaica and ...

ROSE Hmm.

GRMALEM ... you saw that the suffer and the hopes. I'm just like, God! [*Laughs*]

COLE So, you remember that in terms of the feeling of coming from Eritrea?

GRMALEM No, absolutely. Yeah. I'd just been in plane. I've been myself like one time to see my granddad last year, and I was more afraid to go to the plane instead of like going to the desert and all of that, you know?

COLE Yeah.

GRMALEM Because I seen all the crashes and the stuff that, and I was like, how I'm gonna get to the plane? But going to

Sahara, Libya, all that Sudani and stuff, I was like, all I have was hope, you know?

COLE   Mmm.

GRMALEM   All I was thinking, I'm actually like really lucky person, I have to say, from my birth, growing up with my priest granddad.

            All the story of Mary, Joseph, all the story of Abraham, all the story of like, who has not been in refuge? Who has not been, as a Christian, who has not been …? There is no one! Everyone in the Bible has been refuge. Abraham been take away from his family, don't he, and all his family has to live, and Noah, he have to live all his …

COLE   Mmm.

GRMALEM   All of that, I've been taught from my granddad. And Mary. She have to live with, eh, St Mary, great to behold, to remember by me. I mean her love, in Orthodox Christian Coptic as well now as we worship her and we remember, uh, always her suffer. I've been taught that from my granddad. All my journey was like, I deserve this because I'm Christian, you know, I was like saying that as well. I was saying to these people as well with me, I said to them like, right, let's have the hopes as we all our sense have, and then we can survive. And we start praying. We survive as well, because of my granddad, who has taught me all of that.

COLE   You're saying that as you made your journey, which we'll describe in a minute, you had that sense of hope and companionship because of your faith.

GRMALEM   Absolutely. Absolutely. The just like, I haven't been in Abraham's time. I haven't been in Mary's time, Joseph's time, all of that. And you just like, I'm still thinking of how did Mary felt? I was like, how did he survive in Sahara desert? We use a car. Right? But how did … she survived by walking with having a baby?

            Well, he's the greatest God. He can do anything. And she know that as well. He can do anything. But she do not ask to do things except at what times, you know?

COLE	Mmm.
GRMALEM	She was, as like my granddad said, she was so thirsty at one times when she asked, can I have a water from the lady? And he was crying – the God was crying to see his mercy as well. And all my brain was thinking of that as a kid. I was like ...
COLE	Yeah.
GRMALEM	... *how did she survive this?*
COLE	Because these are the stories that you were told.
GRMALEM	These are the stories I've been told.
COLE	And particularly within that tradition, there's that tradition of ...
GRMALEM	Exactly.
COLE	... of Mary being given the water and the plants blooming alongside.
GRMALEM	Yes. Yes.
ROSE	A reminder. A reminder that women are *strong*!
GRMALEM	Exactly! Yes.
ROSE	Yeah!
COLE	Well, here's one, over here! Bridget, what do you make of what you're hearing?
BRIDGET	I have a lot of conversations with people on the Kent coast. There are some people that think that the young people I worked with in the past, they made a choice to come here, that it was an informed choice, they thought about it and they picked this country because we offer a luxury lifestyle for them. And it is so different to the experience of the young people that I worked with. Nobody had a choice.

We've seen recently that the situation in Sudan is really unstable again. A lot of the young people I worked with KRAN were from Sudan. And when they spoke about why they came to the UK, first of all, it was the push factor was great – they weren't safe. But they came here because they said, look, Sudan was a British colony, and we've always been told that this is the mother country. So, of course we came here. Where else would we have gone? And it's a really good question and ... people like Grmalem come from Eritrea, where military conscription is for life; people that I work with from Afghanistan who came because they'd got to an age where they were 14 or so, and the Taliban had turned up and said, 'We're coming to get you next week because you are coming to fight with us.' Again, there's another idea that people coming, not only is it a choice, but they've come because they're fighting-age men, and that they're coming somehow to do damage to our country. And people like Grmalem and the people I work from Afghanistan are coming precisely because they don't want to fight. They want to be safe. They want to live their lives in peace, and they want what we all want, which is community, family, somewhere to call home.

COLE   I'm just reminded of the Warsan Shire quote of the British Somali poet, that nobody leaves home unless home is the mouth of a shark. Such a powerful thing.

GRMALEM   Yes.

COLE   Grmalem, we know that the second time Mary and Joseph had to leave home, they were obviously in a hurry, fleeing King Herod. And we're sharing this picture that Kelly Latimore has made of *La sagrada familia*, which depicts a modern-day holy family. Does that kind of idea speak to you, having been born in one country and lived in the UK now for, what, nine years? Is it?

GRMALEM   Nine years.

COLE   Yes.

GRMALEM   Yeah. So comes, um …

COLE   Has studying here and being in the arts contributed to a feeling of being at home at all here?

GRMALEM   Yes, but as I'm weakest and the scene, I couldn't not compare with Mary and Joseph's been, like in that terrific journeys, but, yes, like, it's all God has made, you know, like Herodas does not compare with what we have in the country. Like Herodas was the kindest person I would say, in thinking of like, what happened my people, like the young people, the young mothers, or like, I do have a picture as well, like I paint, I said I, I name it like a mother who had give seven, nine birth, which she lives alone in a big house now, as we earlier mentioned, you know?

COLE	Mmm.
GRMALEM	She won't see her grandsons, her grandchildrens, all of that, and she can't see that. And who made her that too is one of the new generation Herodas, isn't it?
COLE	Mmm.
GRMALEM	It's just new one. And, of course it does touch me, really, really. But comparing Herodas and my country or my situation is ... Herodas is the kindest person because he did not flew over them to catch Mary and Josephs. He just only sent an army saying, okay, just kill all the children. Right. And John, himself, he hide because he was young as well, with just a six month older, dunnit. All the others was escape as well. Not only just escape, so they do have time to escape. In my country, nobody have. I lost four uncles and my dad has been always in the armies. All the men has lost their lives. Even in the journey, a lot of people has been lost, not just because in the country.
COLE	Yeah.
GRMALEM	It just more than Herodas, the story of Joseph and Mary in the second time, they live because of Herodas?
COLE	Yeah.
GRMALEM	Absolutely. It does touch me and also remember. But, their time was better, I have to say.
COLE	So, so in your case, in Eritrea, you're saying that your dad and others just didn't have time to go, they were just caught up in what was happening.
GRMALEM	Absolutely.
COLE	And lives were lost.
GRMALEM	Absolutely.
COLE	So, when it came to you, what was the situation there and what made you make that decision to go?
GRMALEM	I can see that I'm walking to that dark, as he said, you know, if the home is a shark, as you caught that.
COLE	Yeah.
GRMALEM	You know, it's just, I can see why do I have to jump to the shark, you know? Why do I have to walk to the shark?
COLE	Yeah.

GRMALEM   Why did the young people have to go instead of making plans? As we, Rose Bishop said, we didn't know what is our next step. We just like, right, this is not the step we want.

COLE   Yeah.

GRMALEM   From the country or from ...

COLE   You've just gotta go to escape.

GRMALEM   Exactly.

COLE   Saving your life.

GRMALEM   Saving my life. Just save the body I'm holding.

COLE   What would've happened if you'd stayed?

GRMALEM   There's two things. In God's way, if he wants me, I will be still alive, holding the gun. Like today, I would be fighting. And if, in the other side, I will see myself, I died two years ago because my present was fighting with Tigray region and I will be dead in that and nobody knows where I would be.

COLE   Wow. We're very glad you're here. Bishop Rose, you wanna respond to any of that?

ROSE   When you have moved somewhere, you can either be there or you can be back where you've come from. And there's a real sense in which having journeyed away physically from home, that it's the words of the songwriter, 'Home is where the heart is'. And so you create home, you make home, and that means being given the opportunity and the space to find fellowship and friendship and companionship and food. [Laughs]

COLE   Back to food!

ROSE   Yes. And being able just to sit and eat with food and the people around you and dip. You know, sometimes people say, 'Do you miss Jamaica?' And I say, yeah, I miss Jamaica, but you know, I ... I can go there at some point. This is now home and I am building this home with my family and my friends and the people around me. And I believe that this is my reality.

COLE   Hmm.

ROSE   And it is important. From time to time, I often hear myself thinking, 'If you were back in Jamaica, Rose, what would you be doing?'

I would either have been teaching, or I would've been in the Church's ministry, but I certainly would not be a bishop ... if I was in Jamaica, because there is still a lot of, you know, [*Sings*] 'This is a man's world.' You know, there's a lot of that stuff going on still. I don't think they'd be ready for me as a bishop. [*Laughs*]

COLE   I'm ready for you as a singer, I've gotta tell you, Rose.

Bridget, we got to know each other through the work you were doing with teenagers who'd come across the Channel in small boats, or on lorries, and now you're working with Reset, which helps people to welcome refugees into communities across the country. In your experience, what does home mean to those who are on the move, and also for you, how does living alongside them change your own ideas of home?

BRIDGET   I think home means the same for everybody. I think what I see is that people want somewhere safe to be. They want a community around them. They want to contribute in some way. They'd like some kind of meaningful work. They want their children to be safe. They want their children to be educated. And I think these are just common denominators for everybody, and that's how they build a home.

What I find working with them is a sense of real empathy and compassion at the frustrations that they have because their lives get put on hold for so long. You know, often the people I work with now have been in refugee camps in places like Lebanon, sometimes for seven, eight, nine, ten years, living families in one room unable to access education or meaningful work, and their lives have been on hold. And when I work with the teenagers, often they'd spent three, four, five years making this journey – a painstaking dangerous journey.

And there's a sense of really wanting to get on with it and make up for lost time. And I suppose what I have is an appreciation of the privilege that I have of not having had my life on hold; the fact that when I've wasted time, which I have, it's been my own choice, and the fact that I shouldn't waste time now, that it's a privilege to have that time and to be able to get on with things. So, I think I, you know, it's an immense privilege to work with the people that I work with, and I'm ... I'm grateful for it every day. They are the most amazing bunch, and I just think we're incredibly lucky to have them.

COLE Well, I think we're lucky to have you all round the table today. Thank you for what you've said, and we'll go on and explore some more of these issues in the coming weeks, in the other parts of the course. Thank you.

SESSION 2
FLEEING HOME

COLE　The story tells us that Joseph woke in the night with a burning conviction that he and Mary and the baby should leave in a hurry because they were in danger. There are lots of examples in the Bible, and in other traditions and cultures, of God speaking to people in dreams. So, I'm just wondering around the table, have you ever had that, if you've ever woken from sleep with a deep sense that something needed to be done and did you act on it? Who wants to go first?

GRMALEM　I grew up with the luckiest family, a huge family. My uncle surrounded with his eight, seven kids, also with all animals. I grew up in a farming places, right, and, well, he was in the army and his kid was looking after all the animals and his wife, and same time my family as well, with my mum's side? And my granddad, in between. So, he was ... my granddad was teaching all the kids how to be behave and stuff because his son-in-law and his son was joined the army. And all I was thinking, my brain, I can see my uncle's life, and my daddy's life, even though I'm wake in the day, not just even sleep, I can see all the kids' future is gonna be like that. So, I was always asking God as well, speak to me, one of us, like he speak to all this, sense, but not great too.

COLE　So, asking God to speak to you, like to speak to people in the stories that you were brought up with.

GRMALEM　Exactly. So I can change this kid's life. It's like, I take Moses as an example. He bought his people from Israel across the sea.

COLE　Moses, yeah.

GRMALEM　Moses. All that. I was like, can I be Moses to save this kid to his life?

COLE　Mmm.

GRMALEM　Well, lucky enough, I did have save my family's life because my mum and six brother are here in this country. But, when I was in my country, that was my dream, and that was my wishes to ask God as well.

COLE	Yeah.
GRMALEM	Forget when I was in the journey, I didn't think that [*laughs*], because in the journey I was thinking, I'm gonna die! But when I was at home, I did have that feeling. I did have this feeling and this wishes to do, and God made it real as well. In my sleep, I can see I'm walking Libya? I heard it's the sea. You have to cross the Italy? I didn't see because we didn't have a TV. What I was thinking, the sea is like in between, so we have a rope to walk on? That's what I see in Libya, in my brain. So, if you fell in the rope, you're gonna die.
COLE	Oh, like a tightrope?
GRMALEM	Yeah. Yeah. That's what I was thinking because I didn't know any boats. In my dreams, I can see the Libya sea. It's in rope, so people are in two sides and they pulley down. And I was thinking like, how do I cross that? I can see that in my dream. And, when I ... I finally arrived in Libya, there is a boat and the stuff, I was thinking, oh, this is much easier! [*Everyone laughs.*] So that is all I have in my feeling, and lucky enough, as I said, really great, and with God, and also with the blessing I have, I brought my family to this country.
	As you mentioned, they flew here.
COLE	So the vision, the dream that you had came true.
GRMALEM	It does come true because it's not because if I work for, not because I did things or I just because ... the miracle, greatest love, God. He said that my wishes from my kid, the time I was small. Asking him to do that, to save a small kid who's now always have like learning from his school, you know?
COLE	Mmm.
GRMALEM	To be saved. I ask and I get it. I received as well.
ROSE	Dreams have always played a part ...
GRMALEM	Exactly!
ROSE	... in my life too. And actually, that began my sense of call to ministry. I was in my early teens, I am asleep and in the sleep I had this dream. And in this dream, I couldn't see the, like it's a face that says, you know, it's

Cole, or it's Bridget, or it's, you know, it was a form that says, don't do this or do that. And I'm thinking, wow, this has got to be divine. In my sleep, I'm thinking, this is divine. And at that revelation, I am now being so thankful to God and I'm saying, 'Praise the Lord! Hallelujah! Praise the Lord! For this revelation!' And shouting that woke me up! [*Laughs*] And woke up others in the house! What's going on?

And I'm awake and I'm disturbed. What was that all about? But it is still very vivid in my mind, and so I reach for the Bible. And it falls open at Luke chapter four. 'My eyes saw the Spirit of the Lord is upon me because he has anointed me to preach good news', etcetera, etcetera, etcetera.

Wow! Okay God. All right, I'm gonna go back to sleep now. And the next morning I pick up what was like a *Daily Bread*. It's not called *Daily Bread*, but it's similar to a *Daily Bread* that you read a portion of Scripture and the portion of Scripture allocated for that morning was Isaiah 61, which is actually the Luke version that Jesus read.

So, when Jesus was given the scroll in the Temple, it was the scroll with the words from Isaiah 61. So there again, I'm reading those same words, 'The Spirit of the Lord is upon me'. And it just blew my mind. Something said, 'That's it! You've heard it! You are being called.' And it's a strange thing to be called in a Church that doesn't have women. You know?

COLE   Of course, yes.

ROSE   How do you reconcile that together? So, I made a little pact with God that I would be faithful. 'God, I believe you have called me. I can't see how it's going to unfold, but you have called me. I believe that. I'm going to be faithful and I'm going to leave it with you to work it out with the Church.'

And it took *years*. I was 33 when the Church said yes. And I still listen to my dreams, and they still speak to me in a way that is quite tangible. And I remember them.

COLE   I'm fascinated by this because we all come from different traditions or faith or no faith around the table.

And I've always been really sceptical, to be honest, about dreams and people acting on them. But I'm beginning to be a little bit more convinced. I wanna just slightly move us on.

Bridget, I've got a question for you. I'm always hearing in the news that such and such a number of people have crossed the Channel in small boats on a certain day, and that's a new record. But there's a longer view of this, isn't there? And you've told me a fascinating story about Belgium refugees arriving, I think in Folkstone, drawing out parallels for today. Can you share this with us briefly?

BRIDGET   Yeah, every time I hear a journalist say 'record numbers', my cats have got used to sort of being terrified by my bellow at the radio. It's not record numbers! This, you know, people have always moved. People have always needed to get to safety. In August of 1914, when Germany invaded Belgium, there was conflict. There were explosives going off. There was war. People were displaced because that's what happens when there's conflict. And those people did what we would all do under the circumstances, which is they looked for somewhere safe. And the nearest safe place to be was across the Channel in the UK. And there is a big painting – and I take every visitor that comes to Folkestone and to see it whether they want to or not ...!

COLE   I remember!

BRIDGET   Yeah. [Laughs] They're frog marched to the town museum to see this incredible oil painting, which portrays the great and the good of the town, mostly men it has to be said, I can't remember many women in the crowd, em, this is 1914. So, there's the priest of the town, there's the mayor and the deputy mayor, and all sorts of people in military uniform. And they're welcoming these people that arrived on small boats that have just made that journey across the Channel. And they look cold and semi-hypothermic and wet and tired, exactly as people do when they arrive now. We think in total, figures vary, but local historians think that about 250,000 people came across in a few weeks.

COLE   Wow!

BRIDGET   From Belgium. And on the busiest day, 19,000 people made that journey and arrived into Folkstone.

Population of the town at the time was about 22,000. So, you're talking about effectively doubling the population of the town overnight. So, when people talk now about, you know, being *swamped* by numbers and these very dehumanising words, which I really don't like, 'cause we're talking about human beings ... that town pulled together. People found spare rooms, they found blankets, they made food, they found clothes, and they made sure that everybody had somewhere to sleep, something warm and dry to wear, and something to eat, you know, and they *managed*. And what I say to people is I think we really need to reflect on the fact that we managed to do it then. We're talking actually about far fewer numbers now. And what is different, what has changed? So, we've got a picture of people being welcomed warmly, and now we have people talking about an invasion. And I think people really need to think and have a conversation with themselves about what has changed. I've got my own ideas about that, but I think everybody needs to have their own mental conversation with themselves about that.

COLE   Mmm. Rose, do you wanna say something about that from the perspective of Dover?

ROSE   Yes. The stories that I hear from people are stories about war, stories about civil unrest. So, for example, you have unjust leaders ... where people are hungry for power and they will destroy humanity or places to get to that place of power. And people are saying, 'We can't stay; we have to go.' So, who in their right minds just sits still and say, oh, well, you know, this is happening. Who is going to sit still when there is famine, and you can't feed your family? People are going to pack up, as they did in the biblical times, and move from A to B, to that place where they will find sanctuary, where they're able to feed their family, where they will be at peace. And one of the things that

I hear echo, and you must hear it too, Bridget, people say, oh, they're not real refugees. They are economic migrants.

And I shout at the radio or the television when I hear that because I'm thinking, how dare you? What did you think the British were when they went all over the world? They were economic migrants! The British were trying to make a life, a better life for themselves and their families. That's what empire was all about.

And so, you know, we've been there, done it, and created an attachment with these folks. And so, when something is happening, you think, well, where do we go? Ah, Britain. We know the language, we know the people, you know, their mother country as you said earlier, we are gonna, we are gonna get there.

And I think that it *is* right. You know, this whole world, from my perspective, is God's world. It all belongs to God. And so, everyone has a right to determine, to self-determination and to be able to say to themselves, this isn't working. I can't feed my family. You know? Or, there is war. I need to take my children away from the dangers.

So, I believe that it is the human race's right to self-determination. And what we have done, I think, is that we've created borders. We have created borders, and said, this bit is mine. And that's why we have so many neighbourly wars and things going on across the fence, you know. This is mine, so you don't dare come across it. No, it's not mine. It's actually God's.

COLE   Grmalem, could you describe to us, having had the dream, what the journey entailed?

GRMALEM   Em, well my dream was like, I can see the sea to cross was that narrow?

COLE   Yeah.

GRMALEM   And if one, my body's weight goes to the other side, I would die. That's what I was having a dream. So, I even told my friend that they laugh always, you know, and my journey was quite easy, quiet, clear, quiet. Very, very nice. I'm so amazingly thank to God. In Libya, I stayed a week, where my friend was there for two years. He came travel with me, who I stayed one week. My friend from Sudan, who stayed four years, I travel with him. I stayed in Sudan one day, which my journey was quite ... narrow. But when I reached Libya, I was waiting for the row.

So where is the two people, who's in Italy and who is in Libya to send me away? And only the gun get me shocked because there was, em, Libyan people with a gun who's trying to like, because I don't know the language. I don't know none of these people except the friends I have more than ten, and none of us can speak Arabic. And I couldn't understand when they say to me, 'Move,' or, you know, just even for myself to be safe. And I don't know, they give me bed, but I don't know what they're telling me. They could say to me, 'Eat,' but I don't know what they're saying. And I'm just like standing. And because I'm standing, they just push me with a guns. The action scares me more than the offer of the word. You know? I was just like, oh God. And when I see both I was like, oh, my dream is froth. My dream was not real.

COLE   So how did you finally get to Britain?

GRMALEM   Well, illegal. [Laughs] I came Britain from France. I stayed six weeks in Calais ... every second ... the time ... I've tried ... lorries, cars, even in people's boots car, you know, it's just like in the driver seats – everywhere. The only place I didn't go is a break side of the cars. I did not have hopes to come to England, but I just was looking for a place that I can be saved and save brothers, sisters, anybody I can save.

COLE   You are talking about doing things that really risked your life ... for a place that you didn't know anything about. So then, what was driving you?

GRMALEM   The life I'm breathing; my breath was pushing me to be saved. The only, my body was dead.

COLE   And you thought that England was a place where you would be saved?

GRMALEM   That is what I thought.

COLE   Rose, while we are hearing that and rejoicing that Grmalem is safe and has a place to live, we also have to acknowledge, don't we, that there are people here who are uncomfortable with the situation that's happening around them. Pope Francis says that as Christians we should think of Jesus in the arms of Mary and Joseph as they fled, and see him in each of the migrants of today. That's quite a challenge though for the people of a town like Dover, isn't it, where there's such a situation happening? And not to mention any community or nation. So how is that working out?

ROSE   I think it is important that we do not forget that aspect of it. The, the reality is, and in particular, I mean I'm addressing those who are within the Church, for example, because there are many within the Church, and I say the Church of England because this is what I know, who are critical.

I had someone ... When we had folks dying, the second group of people that died crossing the Channel, I went on to the media and I said, you know, these people are our mothers and fathers and brothers and sisters. And I got a letter from someone who said, 'How dare you say that? I am an Evangelical Christian! They are not our mothers and fathers and brothers and sisters. They are Muslims!'

I usually ignore such letters, but I wrote back so fast and I said, 'I am ashamed to be in this space with you called Christian.' I feel that I have a responsibility, not just because I'm a bishop, but because I'm a child of God, to say to the people of God, the Christ who we worship was himself a refugee.

And we don't think of that, you see. We like to think of this wonderful story, you know, and we leave off the roughness of it and the challenges that Mary faced. As a woman who've had a baby, I don't want to be in a stable! You know, I want to be in a posh room, which is *clean*!

COLE   To be fair.

ROSE   Yes. So, what I want to do as a child of God is actually to give a message that says, *we belong*.

So, you *are* my brother, you *are* my sister, whatever your country of origin is. And might I just pause and say, what if I was in your shoe? What if, you know, those bombs or those challenges or there's food scarcity – what if those things were happening? How would I like someone to respond to me on arrival? And I think that what we are seeing is a failure for us to stand in each other's shoe.

And I think that there is a responsibility for those of us, lay and ordained, who belong to the faith to reflect this back to each other. And also, there's an education that is needed because a lot of people here don't know their history. They don't know that the British went all over the world kicking behinds and claiming places and people and, you know, 'We are in charge!' Hey!

Well, we are reaping some of that cause you *heard* about Britain and what it may have done, you didn't *know* it. And so, that is one of the reasons. It has nothing to do with people thinking they're gonna be put up in hotels. I mean, that's something different and has to do with our inability as government to govern the people or ordinary people: they're hungry, they're thirsty. Were you there? In as much I was hungry, I was thirsty, you gave me nothing to drink. Nothing to eat. I was naked. You did not clothe me. I was sick in prison. You did not visit me. And of course, Oh, but if we'd *seen* you! Bridget! You are my mate – of course I would've done this to you. Aha!

But in as much as you have not done it to Grmalem, and you haven't done it to Bridget, you haven't done it to your mothers, and you have not done it to me. So, it's about how do we learn? And how do we teach? How do we practise what it means to reach out and touch and show love, and give love and warmth and welcome?

COLE   Thank you. And we will go on to explore these themes, which are touching us all around the table now, in the coming weeks. But for now, thank you very much.

CARRYING HOME

COLE	Hello again. The Travelling Light exhibition by my friend Kiki Streitberger photographed the contents of people's bags, after they'd crossed the sea to Germany, and recorded their words. Could you briefly say what you'd take if you had to flee quickly and why? And I know, Grmalem, that's quite relevant to you 'cause you did have to! So, let's start with you.
GRMALEM	Nothing. I did have hopes, faiths ... all the spirit thing. Not that's something I will have it for the next day. I mean, I mean like in physical. Em, but all I have was like the dream, and the ... God actually, just him, the big man ... like the greatest, you know, um, I have him. And that was everything.
COLE	That was it.
GRMALEM	So, I didn't have spare things.
COLE	You just went. No time to pack a bag? Nothing.
GRMALEM	No, no, nothing. I wrote a number in my belt to remember my auntie's number.
COLE	A telephone number.
GRMALEM	Telephone number.
COLE	Okay.
GRMALEM	'Cause I couldn't put anything in my pocket. And it just, I didn't change, I didn't have a shower, I didn't nothing in my pocket because even when it gets sweat and stuff and they get not comfortable when they sit down, no papers, no pens even. It's just *nothing* I can bring. The only thing I can bring is was something I can cover myself and just go for it.
COLE	So your only connection with anybody else was that number that was written inside your belt.
ROSE	There's something quite biblical about that. When Jesus was sending the disciples out and he says, take nothing with you, just this, and that does what you need. Because we often are weighed down ... with *stuff*! [*Laughs*]
COLE	Yeah. I guess they had a choice though. That's, that's the difference there.

ROSE   Yes. Yes. But you know, you talk about what you carry. This little book, it's uh, my little book, Common Prayer book, which was given to me by my daddy, my adopted dad when, uh, I was leaving Jamaica. I was 18 years old. And you can see it's all worn, but I still have it with me. I still carry it with me. And Daddy wrote in it. He put my name in it and it had a quote from John 4:8: 'God is love.' You know, so even if I don't get to read any of the other bits, I can see that 'God is love'. Propels me.

COLE   And actually the love that he had for you was carried in the book, right?

ROSE   Oh, yes. Oh, yes.

COLE   I can see it in your eyes, right? Yeah. I wanted to ask this question because of seeing Kiki's exhibition and seeing what people had brought, and obviously, in a similar situation, they weren't able to bring much at all.

But there were just these tiny things. There was a guy who'd had a shop, a supermarket that was his own supermarket in Iran, I think, and he'd brought the lighter that had the branding of the shop on it. And the lighter didn't work any more, hadn't worked for a long time. But the fact that it had the branding of *his* shop on it reminded him that he had had that shop in Iran.

But the one that really got me was ... there was a teenager, I think he was 13 or 14. And he had come from Afghanistan, I think, and he had carried with him his school report. And they asked him why, and he said, 'Because I was good in my class, and I want people to know wherever I go that I'm not stupid. Because they have ideas about me because I've come across the water or because I'm a migrant, but I want them to see my school report and know that I'm not stupid.'

Bridget, one of the reasons I guess, for asking this question and getting people to think about it at home, is also just to put ourselves in that position. What would it be like for us? What would I take? I've been giving a lot of thought to it, in fact ... I mean, if I didn't have time to take anything, as Grmalem has said, you know, that would be frightening, very frightening. What do you make of all this?

BRIDGET   I was really interested in what you just said about the kid from Afghanistan that brought his school report because he wanted people to know that he was good. And I've worked with hundreds of young people like Grmalem, who are all incredible bundles of potential. And I'm frustrated all of the time because we are missing out on so much talent because we don't put enough language support in place for the people arriving. You know, just because somebody's English level is at a certain level, often their intellectual level is right up here.

So we're not matching the two and enabling them to move forward and achieve to their fullest potential, which is not only better for them, but much better for, for all of us. And I'm thinking of a, a woman I've worked with who arrived as an adult who's ... was a fully qualified midwife in Syria, and would love to go back to work as a midwife in this country – and we *need* midwives – and hasn't got the language support to enable her to requalify in this country. So, one of the things I'm thinking, first of all, is just of my immense frustration and the fact that with a few tweaks we could be mining a wealth of talent that we are just missing out on at the moment. And it's really, really, really rubbish for us as a country, but it's really, I think, such a waste of lives that are full of potential.

In terms of what people bring with them ... you know, a lot of the time, the one thing that I see in the, the papers and the media that people complain about is that people have got a mobile phone. It makes me laugh. It's ... when ... if you ask me what I would bring with me, if I had to go at short notice, it would be my phone.

And it would be my phone because it's the way I communicate with people. It's my camera. It stores all my photographs, all of my memories. It's got my music on it. I listen to the radio and I tend to listen to the radio through my phone these days.

ROSE   And you probably have the voices of your loved ones on it.

BRIDGET I have. I have everything on it. I have absolutely everything on this. And I cannot understand the kind of psychology of somebody that says, 'You know, well, if you have a mobile phone, you can't possibly be a refugee.' I remember somebody arriving on a boat and somebody thought they'd spotted an expensive watch on their wrist and said, 'You know, he can't possibly be a refugee, I think he's got a Rolex on,' as if somehow wealth protects you from bombs and from being persecuted. I don't understand this. And it, it goes along with that idea of people being economic migrants. They've *chosen* to make this journey.

ROSE   And it's also the comment that I hear too, that says, 'Well, how did they afford to, to pay for the people smugglers to get here? They, you know, they can afford ...' I mean, they don't understand that in those cases, families will get together.

BRIDGET Yeah, yeah.

ROSE   And they will pool and send one who is strong, who they think will make it. And, you know, the trust that they put there so that that person can then later on help the next one and the next one, and it's money's gotta be paid back.

COLE   We've talked about how those memories and those connections with people can make us feel at home. Other people also have things that they're running from in their heads. You know, they have mental baggage that they, they want to leave behind. Whatever our circumstances in life, we're all sharing this longing for safety and security and love. And that also goes for the people who are welcoming or not welcoming people to their own communities in this country.

         So, a lot has been said about the welcome extended, or not, to refugees in Britain. Bishop Rose, you've been an outspoken and compassionate voice on this. Can you share some of your thoughts about that, about the way people are being received, but also, you know, you were Chaplain to the Speaker of the House of Commons. In general, without getting into any individuals – you might want to, but let's not – how would you reflect on the way our communities and our politicians are dealing with these issues?

ROSE   What is interesting for me ... when the government said, 'We're putting it out there, if people want to receive Ukrainians,' and the thousands of people who desperately said, 'Yes, we will. We will have them.' What that signalled to me is that the vast majority of people in our country are compassionate. But then we have a small minority, and they are a small minority, but they're loud and they give the impression as if they are in greater numbers. And what we have today, and over the years, are different colours of government, who decides, that because these people are so loud about why we got these immigrants coming to our country and changing the nature of who we are, etcetera, the government decides, instead of doing the right thing, successive governments have actually decided, *chosen* to play a game. But the game that they're playing is quite dangerous. Because what they're doing, they are almost outcompeting each other in saying, look how, you know, we are good at securing our boundaries and keeping our people safe and keeping people out.

It's a dangerous game, because as more than one parliamentarian reminded me when I was chaplain in Parliament, 'Rose, you know that, you know, after we've had this debate and we may have had our big row in the chambers, you know, we go back to the tearoom or to the, you know, to have drinks together.' I said, 'Yes, but the people in the various communities, they don't see that. I see that and I know that. So, you have a responsibility as political leaders to set the right *tone* ... that is necessary for there to be harmony and compassion in our communities.'

So, what I would personally like to see from our governments, of whatever colour, I want them first of all to say, 'Yes, this is a challenge for us.' But there's an even greater challenge, greater than, you know, where do we put people, etcetera. And that challenge is, to ask the question, why are people fleeing Eritrea, the Sudan, Yemen, Nigeria or wherever else they're coming from? And to dare to ask those questions of those governments as well. What is happening? Not to ask in a judgemental way, but to say, 'Actually, you know, we still have a human responsibility as part of the human race, not because we are colonial masters anymore, but because we share a common humanity. Something is going wrong. Your people are hungry. They tell us they're hungry. They tell us they're fleeing war. How can we assist?' How can we assist in those places? How can we perhaps stop selling weapons because we want to boost our economy here? To unscrupulous world leaders who are going to use it on their own people, how can we stop doing that?

How can we help to create local industry that is going to enable A and B to find work and feed their family? How can we do that? So that's what they need to do. Instead, they're pulling out dead people from the Channel. And saying, but why are they coming across? That's too late. Catch them before they jump into the Channel, before they jump into the smugglers' vehicles that are taking them. And we can do that. But you know what? There is no political will. All we are doing is stirring up, on the ground, animosity.

COLE   Which creates people who say, you're wrong or you're stupid, or whatever. There are people who are presumably coming to you as a bishop as well, and to both of you as well, who're saying, 'Look, I get that these people have need, but I'm frightened. I feel overwhelmed. I don't understand where these people are coming from or why they're here, and it scares me. I wish they weren't.' We can't just bat that away, can we? That's a genuine concern. So what do we say to that?

ROSE   I don't want us to bat that away, but this morning on the news, I was devastated when I heard the story of a 16-year-old boy who had gone to knock on someone's door to get his brother.

COLE   In America, yeah?

ROSE   In America. It just so happened that he knocked on the wrong door. And so, the occupant of the house didn't just see a young boy. He saw someone who he *feared*. Teenager, 16-year-old boy, who was a good student – not a tearaway on the street – and shot him twice. So, I want to ask. As a little girl, growing up in Jamaica, we were inundated with white people. Loads of them!

The cruise ship pulls in and they're pouring into Montego Bay. I never once felt afraid. I never once felt, why are they coming to our country? What is wrong with white people, I must ask myself the question. Why are you afraid of black people? Why is it that it never occurred to the government that the same way that they ... I said, 'Let's ask people to throw open their homes to accommodate Ukrainians.'

Why haven't they done that for black people and pink people and blue people? There's a real issue there. They're human beings, and it is because, and that's the underlying problem, because we do not see ourselves in each other. We see them as strangers. They're, you know, they're asylum seekers, they're migrants. Then we can afford to treat them in a way that says they are not as we are. We're human. They're a little less than human. And that's ... you can only be afraid of something that is not like you.

BRIDGET   Yeah. I think the government need to be much more temperate with the language that they use. I think that using words like invasion are deeply ...

ROSE   And swamping ...

BRIDGET   ... deeply irresponsible and dehumanising.

First of all, we can't make people afraid that everybody's going to come here. That's just not true. Secondly, if we're part of an international community, we have a duty to step up and take our fair share, you know, that's really, really important. And thirdly, if we want people to stay in the region that they came from, which most of them are already doing, then we've got to do what Bishop Rose just talked about, which is talk

	to governments abroad and work with them and try to mitigate the conflict that's driving them out. We also don't do it by cutting the aid budget …
ROSE	Yeah.
BRIDGET	… which we've just done.
ROSE	Yes.
BRIDGET	You know, you can't live it both ways. You can't say, 'Well, we're not going to enable you to stay in your region. But you can't come here either.' I mean, that's just morally bankrupt, and …
ROSE	And we haven't, we haven't mentioned climate change, right? Because when that hit in an even bigger way, it's already impacting. That's gonna be even worse. People are going to move.
BRIDGET	Yeah.
COLE	Bridget, what we are seeing, and you're seeing through the charity Reset, is that people are being compassionate and they are opening their homes. Tell us briefly about that.
BRIDGET	Yeah, so what Bishop Rose was talking about, people coming from Ukraine and being hosted by people in this country, we work on that programme, Homes for Ukraine. We also work on a programme called Community Sponsorship, which I just think is the most brilliant, brilliant thing that so many people in this country don't know about. And it's my mission at the moment through work to spread the word about Community Sponsorship. 'Cause what Community Sponsorship does is it enables groups of people to come together. And they have a process they need to go through. And that process is not an easy process. It can take between a year and two years. They have to tick a number of different boxes. But once they've done that, they can then sponsor a refugee family to come from a camp in somewhere like Lebanon, to come to the UK, to a house that is ready, on a plane, with paperwork, not getting in a dinghy, to a house that's ready for them. Nothing special, you know, not jacuzzis in the back garden, nothing like that! Just a small house that they can come to that is theirs, and

where they've got a community around them that is there to support as they find their feet in this new country. And I believe that there is huge potential in this country to expand that scheme.

And let me tell you that to me, it's amazing because any company that comes through the Community Sponsorship scheme – that's over and above any numbers that the government, small numbers, that the government have already agreed to take – so every family that comes through that route is a family that would've been stuck otherwise in limbo, not able to get on with their lives.

So, I just think that that is, in terms of home and in terms of being welcoming, that is a way of offering people a safe route and a way of integrating them into our communities and everybody is gonna benefit from that.

COLE   Grmalem, what was your experience when you came here? Were people welcoming to you and also at that time, how did your faith help with that?

GRMALEM   Ahh ... it's two things. Em, thanks to God, the Methodist Church, Canterbury, St Peter, for the seven years we are using this, the church as like my house. And ...

BRIDGET   You worship there.

GRMALEM   We worship there in the building. You know, sometime we, well even in Bible said, as Peter, God is everywhere, and God is in you. In me, in the house, outside, everywhere. But especially in the St Peter's Church. He is there, the Father, the Son, the Holy Spirit. And when I go there, *everything* is just like ready, and I'm so grateful.

COLE   That's the gathering of people from your community.

GRMALEM   That is where I gather for this eight years. And where that I start building my communities, where I give the young people encourage to stay in their faith and in their cultures, and just try to bring their memory a bit because they do not have nothing. They do not have their mother's voice, their brothers or their sons or their wife, so they can just barely hear it, this kind of memory. Comparing what they just say now, Ukrainian

... Every house in this country have got the Ukrainian flag! That example, when you go to airport, you welcome your wife or your sons, you never sing, what did he take with you? Flowers and something transport. If you didn't take the flowers or nothing, it kind of, you're not welcoming too much, are you? Putting the flag of Ukrainian, and putting nothing for us, that is how I felt. I was like seeing the flag everywhere in the UK now. It makes me like, wow!

BRIDGET Yeah.

GRMALEM But St Peter, in Canterbury ... Because I just kind of don't want to see them ... I have to thank them so much, even in my word, because they get from God. But also, they have to hear – this just is so amazing. But others, also my foster was welcoming as well. My foster is a Christian believer in Folkestone, and at the time I was praying in a toilet. My first prayer was in toilet. So, every time I went out, said, 'Mum, I need to pray.' Because the knowledge of prayer is in my brain. I do not need a book how to ask God; how to speak God. I just need the space that I can speak to God. And she's like, 'Yes, let's go ... to our church.'

When I go to their church, because they have got their own service as well, so I go to the disabled toilet, and I do my prayers. I do my conversations with God. And I did hear him as well. So, from that I moved to the St Peter Church. Now, days and nights I spend there without using the, like didn't, no pay, nothing. I do not even pay for the weathers, electrics, nothing.

COLE So they welcome you in then.

GRMALEM They welcome me so much. God welcome me so much.

COLE Thank you. There's plenty there to discuss and to think about and to be moved by and angered by, and ... we have one more session in which we'll talk about finding home, but for now, thank you.

SESSION 4
FINDING HOME

COLE	So we know Jesus says that those who want to follow him need to leave their home and family. Bishop Rose, when you'd come from Montego Bay, Jamaica, to here, and you had a poster given to you at college that read, 'Do not go where the path leads; instead go where there is no path and leave your own' – how has that had an impact on your understanding of home?
ROSE	D'you know, the words from that poster, they resonated with me and have done so for all the years that I have now lived here in this country. Because there is something about, how do we ... as we go through life, certain things are thrown at you. Someone once said, if you are given only lemons, what do you do with it? You make lemonade. You don't just sort of, 'Oh, yuck,' and throw it away. You make something of it. And so for me, what that poster did was just to remind me that there are certain pathways you can follow in other people's footsteps, or you can carve out, from your life. You know, you don't need to throw your hands up in despair and think, oh my goodness, is this all? But, what can I do with this that I have been given? I used to have a wonderful elderly nun called Sister Francis, and I've got a painting of her above my door, my study door, and I look up at her and we have this conversation. Because she always said to me, whenever she heard me saying, oh, you know, 'If I was in Jamaica ...,' she would stop me. She said, 'Rose, this is your reality – deal with it!'
COLE	Hmm.
ROSE	So now, I tell that to myself. This is my reality and I will deal with it. 'God is in this reality,' as my brother said, God being everywhere. And if God is here and present, then I am going to make sure that the life that I live is going to be in abundance. And not in abundance in terms of *stuff*, but in abundance in terms of the *quality of relationships* that we build, because

that's what's important. How do we enable the young child growing up to feel that they belong, that this is theirs, this is their home. And that they can carve out a path for themselves. How do we get them to dream, and to see? And for me, if faith was not a part of that story, I would not have had the strength to stay on track, to create a trail, to carve out my own path.

So I'm, I'm very lucky that I was able to stay close to that person who called me initially. And you know, in the past people have said, 'Why have you kept going here in the UK, in the Church?' And I used to say, 'Because I know who called me.' And that makes a difference. So, without my faith, I cannot see I would be here having this conversation with my sister and my, my brother. Without my faith, I would not have climbed the mountains that I have climbed or even *believe* that I can climb the mountain top, and actually to go down into the valley and not be afraid of the valley.

COLE   Mmm.

ROSE   But to build community, and to create a new trail for that next generation, ah, to come along to say, 'Actually I'm gonna start out on this trail, and maybe I too will carve out a new path.'

COLE   Mmm. Thank you. Bridget and Grmalem, any reflections on what Bishop Rose has said?

GRMALEM   I'll ask Bishop Rose, it just because, it's quite different, you know, I don't leave my country because of God is faith or the faith that I would like Noah's Ark, you know …

COLE   You had to go.

GRMALEM   … or Abraham, you know. My story's quite different because Herodas were there, you know, someone has to force me, you know? But how for you, like, would you leave now this country if Herodas came say and say to you, 'Leave this.' And then this country, as we said, 'cause we don't know, if we open the door and the war will start, would you leave this country?

ROSE   I'm always ready. I'm always ready. I live this life to God. And so, growing up within the faith, I learned obedience. Not because other people taught me the obedience, but it was the obedience of Mary, who said yes. It was the obedience of Joseph, who also said yes. He wanted to do something different! But, he said yes. And so, as I read Scripture and see the abundance of life, once people were obedient, then I want to be obedient to that still small voice. So yes, I will be ready to go.

COLE   You make a great point though, in your particular circumstances, making that parallel with the story of Mary and Joseph and Jesus, it was for you as if Herod had sent his soldiers, right, to come and get you, that you had to go in order to avoid being forcibly conscripted into the army, in order to avoid horrors of that situation. Therefore, if you have been forced to leave, in that way, and you find yourself in another country that you don't know, in the early days, how do you begin to say, 'Okay, this is my home now'?

GRMALEM   In the Sahara, when we leave Khartoum, Sudan, the capital city, one night journey, there was storming. The sun was like, really ... you, I could not see my foot where it lands, and once it lands, it's a hole, wherever the sun's moved. And people are sick. I just walk over them. And I fall over. Once I fall over, the sun comes over me and just hidden ... All the people was that night was hidden until the next. So the shout the people were saying the storm was sounding as well like fhhhhhhhhhh. All of that was so scary.

So I said to the people, 'Neighbour, let's stand to pray.' It's not actually three because it's, but it's smaller, bit higher than the sun. It just, just tiny bit. I said, 'Let's go stand next to it and stand to pray. That could be our house to pray to Lord.' And we stand there. I'm talking really serious. Everything calm down, all except the stuff some people carriage, or the clothes. Nobody lost from us. Nobody go away. The storm goes, everything comes down. Every time we stand that place now, we did pray and we make a house. If I have to leave my country in the forced way, I will make somewhere a house for myself, as I did in England as well. Well, in Canterbury, I have got my own community, saying like the Coptic Orthodox Church, Eritrean and Ethiopian. 'Cause I couldn't, I wish I speak another language, I could make it, but because I only speak these two languages, I just having that beliefs or that faith is … still makes me, and I'm still grateful for God as well, making that happen. I wish I could be the saint to live because of God makes me to live in others' beliefs or faiths, but in my way of weakness and strength, I will do.

COLE   In both these true stories, uh, in your story, Rose, and your story, Grmalem, there's been a continuity of sorts, even in the most difficult circumstances that faith and community have come together. So, you can be part of the Church here and you can be part of your church community here too.

Bridget, I want to ask you this. You've been in contact with many people who are making similar changes and even more dramatic changes as well. And for many of them, there isn't that sense of continuity … necessarily. So, how have you seen it from your perspective in terms of embracing the life stories of people with very different backgrounds as you've worked with them? How have you seen them finding their feet and finding senses of home in a new place?

BRIDGET   One of the things that we tried to do at KRAN is … well, we said that we could never replace people's family, but we wanted to be a sort of second family somewhere that people could come and there was always a place for them. There was always a friendly smile. There was always somebody to ask how you were doing. And that, I think, is just incredibly important that to, to feel welcomed in a place, to feel that there are people that care about you; that are looking out for you. I mean, we did all sorts of things. We provided English language classes. We did cooking classes.

I think what a lot of people don't know but … if you arrive in this country as an unaccompanied asylum-seeking child, if you are 16 or 17 and you are a boy, you're not going to end up in foster care. What's gonna happen to you is a few of you are gonna be placed together in a house. There won't be an adult present in that house, and you will be left to get on with it, essentially. And so, in my time at KRAN, I've come across all sorts of things. I remember being called because somebody said they had no lights in the house, and when I got round there, they'd been sitting in the dark and the cold in February for about two days because the electricity had run out on the key, and nobody had shown them how to top it up.

So, what we tried to do at KRAN was to try and enable people to be as successful as possible in the situations in which they found themselves. We couldn't magic up foster carers for them. But we could give them cooking lessons, and we could teach them some of the mysteries of British culture – like what goes into recycling bin, 'cause, heaven only knows, I can't work it out. Does the Tetra pack go in or not? I dunno! You know, we had whole lessons on things like, who knocks on my door? Because you know, if you're a teenager and you've got people knocking on the door, and you don't know whether it's a rogue salesperson, somebody soliciting your vote, a Jehovah's Witness, you know, there's all sorts of reasons and you are left to deal with that. So, we would try and give people the knowledge and the skills to deal with that, and to be happy, healthy and successful. But the most important thing I think we did, and I think this is something that everybody can do, is to make sure that people that have arrived in your community have somewhere to go where somebody is warm and welcoming to them, because that is just invaluable.

ROSE   I think it's so important that we encourage, *practically*. It's no good only saying, 'Let's pray for them.' You know, we need, we need more than the prayer.

BRIDGET   Yeah.

ROSE   We need that physical warmth. We need that welcome. We need those individuals who are there to know that if they're in pain or ... that there is a door that they can knock on, there's someone, a number that

they can call to say, help, or, how do I do this or ...
yeah, it's so important. So, I think within our churches,
which are communities in their own right, we need to
encourage that spirit of welcome in a really practical
way.

BRIDGET   Yeah.

ROSE   And also, we sometimes need to be voices for them, to
speak up if we see young people on the street being
accosted or whatever. Or even here, our friends and
families, speaking in a derogatory manner about those
who are coming to our country, we need to have the
courage to say, 'What do you mean by that?' and
'Why have you said that?' and, you know, 'Do you not
believe they're humans?'

COLE   I just want to say for those listening, that KRAN that
we've been talking about is Kent Refugee Action
Network, which is helping a lot of people, and there
are similar charities across the country doing similar
things.

   You also talked in previous sessions, Grmalem,
about how St Peter's in Canterbury has helped you in
terms of hosting your church community, and I know
that you've just been on this epic journey to celebrate
Easter with people in Leeds and Middlesborough, is
that right?

GRMALEM   Yes. Scarborough.

COLE   Scarborough as well ... to go and see people. And
also, you've just been learning art and studying. So,
there's a sense of a number of different communities for
you, being welcoming.

   Therefore, I'd like to ask you, and indeed Bridget
and Bishop Rose, as people are listening to this, and
thinking, what can we do? How can we make those
who come to the UK feel more at home, where would
you start? What would you say to them?

GRMALEM   I have to say that, first of all, is also not just for the
people who's welcoming. I say to people, as myself, I
do not go to church just to receive something. I go to
church to give something as well. Like saying to God,
I'm giving you this hymns today, myself. I will use a

computer to write this song. The people can joy and sing for you. So that is my job. I can offer to God and he give me strength for that so I can ... the people joy with the sings, they joyed and he happy because of their joy.

COLE   So you're giving away.

GRMALEM   So I am giving away also to receive his bless of his love. So, in the way that I also say to young people, we not just wanted them to welcome us. We have to give something to get what we wanted also.

COLE   Mmm.

GRMALEM   God said in some point, you do not get nothing if you love the ones you ...

ROSE   Oh yes!

GRMALEM   ... they loved. If you love the one who hates you, is the one who get loved. So it just that. I didn't give nothing. Just love me as I am, and that is where you can get the blessed, and that is where you can get the most of it.

So, all the support I have from my foster, all the support I have from my St Peter's Church, I go joy them their services. I go to, as I said, I went to Scarborough, Leeds, all over. I just ... I give them my smile, I give them my welcome. I give them all of that, and they give me back much, much, much more that because I am the one who needed help.

COLE   Yeah. I'm really interested that you are now responding to all this by volunteering again with KRAN. Because one of the things that really spoke to me as I was writing the notes was this question of, is it a home if you don't open it up? Is it a home if you don't give it away, you know, if you don't let people in and let them know they're welcome?

So, as we finish, Bridget and Rose, what can we do to make that happen?

BRIDGET   I would say that ... I imagine many of the people listening to this will say, we're in favour of refugees. We support refugees. But I think that people have to be really proactive in that support. They have to really get out there and show that. Prayers are wonderful. Donations to charity are fantastic. But I think that we have to be having those difficult but respectful conversations with people that are saying negative things about refugees. We have to be challenging our elected representatives politely, but *robustly*, in saying that they don't ... that's not what we stand for.

We want to see kindness and decency and humanity. It's not enough just to sort of quietly drop a fiver in occasionally and say a few prayers. We have to really show ... I mean, what would Jesus have done? I think Jesus would be on the beaches with a warm blanket and a flask of coffee, making sure that people knew that they were welcome, being actively welcoming, and I think that's really, really important.

I think that people can find a refugee charity near them. There will be one. Spend some time, it can be an hour or two, that's all. Volunteer with them at Kent Refugee Action Network, KRAN. They run a mentor programme where people give up an hour or two a week. And they're matched with a person that's arrived as an unaccompanied asylum-seeking child.

There's a lot of safeguarding built in, obviously. But it gives that person yet another adult who's on their side, and who can help them understand letters they've had from the Home Office that might be frightening; help them with bit of homework they've had from college; help them with their aspirations in life.

'Cause we all rely on a bit of, you know, oh, I know somebody that can help out with that, don't we? We all rely on friends and contacts, and these are people that don't have that kind of social network. So, you can absolutely share that with other people. And if you really want a challenge, I would ask you to look at Community Sponsorship and actively see if you can work with a group of people to bring a family to safety in this country. So there's a few things I'd encourage you to do.

ROSE   And you know, at the end of most of our services, especially if it is a service that has holy communion with the bread and the wine, we say this prayer that has these words in it: 'Send us out, in the power of your Spirit, to live and work to your praise and to your glory.'

So the, the coming together for worship ought not to be a holy, you know, a holy stuff that you do and that's it. You go through the door and it's forgotten. 'Send us out in the power of your Holy Spirit to live ...' We've gotta live what we have been hearing from the gospel and being preached from the gospel.

So, in other words, what folks must not say is, 'We can't hear what you're saying because of what I see you doing or not doing.' So, we've got to live it, and we've gotta work it there. It's gotta be real, what we've heard and read in Scripture, we've got to make it real in the lives of the communities where we live. And we need to be saying to our politicians, what you are saying and the way you are behaving, *not in my name, not in my name.*

We need to encourage people to reflect on what is being done politically and said politically and how does it compare with what Jesus ask of us? And what Jesus ask of us, is that we become our brother's and sister's keeper. And for me that holds together the sense of, you know, every week we stand and say, 'We are the body of Christ.' That we does not exclude those who are coming, looking for sanctuary in our countries.

COLE   Thank you. What a great place to finish. Rose, Bridget, Grmalem, thank you so much for sharing what you have with us. I'm sure that people will really want to respond, and if you are listening and watching, thank you for doing that and for following the study notes as well. And I hope you've got something from it.

So, from all of us, thank you and goodbye.

COLE MORETON is an award-winning writer and broadcaster who has written for *The Guardian, The Telegraph* and many other publications. He makes documentaries for BBC Radio 4 and was named Interviewer of the Year at the Press Awards for his work with the *Mail on Sunday*. Cole lives near Beachy Head on the south coast of England and spends as much time as possible staring out to sea. His debut novel, *The Light Keeper*, was highly praised, while his newest book *Everything Is Extraordinary* (Hodder) explores encounters with remarkable people. Cole would like to thank the Revd Jessica Foster for her invaluable collaboration on this project.

ROSE HUDSON-WILKIN CD, MBE is Bishop of Dover and was formerly Chaplain to the Speaker of the House of Commons.

BRIDGET CHAPMAN is a campaigner who advocates for refugees in Kent, and is now with Reset, a charity that supports communities to welcome refugees through schemes such as Community Sponsorship.

GRMALEM GONETSE KASA came to the UK from Eritrea a number of years ago and is currently studying Fine Art at university in Canterbury.

York Courses: https://spckpublishing.co.uk/bible-studies-and-group-resources/york-courses